SPAIN BRASIL MOSES & COLTRANE

Africa Redefined

BY

E. GERONIMO ROBINSON,

C.A.S., FAAIDD

Spain, Brasil, Moses & Coltrane: Africa Redefined

Text copyright © 2024 Geronimo Robinson
All Rights Reserved.

Manufactured in the United States of America.

All rights reserved. No part of this book may be used or reproduced in any capacity without written permission except in the case of brief quotations intended for use in critical articles and reviews.

In the event that you use or enact any of the material in this book, the author and publisher assume no responsibility for your actions.

The publisher, Lightning Fast Book Publishing, assumes no responsibility for any content presented in this book

Summary: Spain, Brasil, Moses & Coltrane: Africa Redefined is a book that examines that glaring presence of African culture globally.

ISBN: 979-8-9882743-4-6

www.lfbookpublishing.com
http://www.lfbookpublishing.com

To my daughters Maya and Lea.
I love you both with all my heart, and
both of you are my light and my life.
I am honored to be your dad and
be a part of your journey of life.

A NUBIAN WOMAN BECAME ONE WITH THE NILE;
WOMBED, NOURISHED AND BLEW THE
BREATH OF LIFE INTO THE FIRST SENTIENT
HOMO SAPIEN BEING.

The Foreword

People of all ethnic and cultural backgrounds who are interested in Black American history and civilization need to understand that we have a direct connection to ancient African peoples, such as the Kemites and Nubians that originated in what we (Afro-centric scholars) categorize as equatorial Africa (as opposed to North Africa, where Arabs now inhabit).

In the past, Black historians sought to establish who we are, and point out leaders of note who have made a profound impact on American and world events. But now the time has come to take this philosophical approach to the next level. The time has come to not only recognize our greatness, and the greatness of our ancestors; we must begin to redefine the parameters of our greatness, reposition ourselves to enable us to take back those civilizations that were colonialized by the ancient ones, and recognize: the direct connection of the musica do Brasil, and the religions of Brasil to the music of West Africa and the religions that originated in the Motherland, the direct connection of the architecture of Spain to the architects and urban planners of Northwestern and North Central Africa, the direct spiritual, theological, and cultural connection of Moses and Israel to Kemite and Canaan, and understand that the history of the Hebrew tribes and Africa are inextricably intertwined, the direct connection between the development of American culture and the contributions of African American scholars, composers, scientists and musicians such as John Coltrane to that culture.

Table of Contents

Foreword...v

I.   Introduction...1

II.   The Process 5

III.   Who's Black and who's not.......................................9

IV.   The list of 10 most prevalent Myths about Africa...................15

V.   The top 4 Countries of the world influenced by Africa:.........27

VI.   **Spain** 29

VII.   The Moors: The Black African Tribe that Africanized Spain ..33

VIII.   The Moors "list" of achievements..............................39

IX.   Top 4 countries in Europe influenced by Africa 41

X.   **Brasil** 47

XI.   Other Countries in Central and South America
        influenced by Africa...53

XII.   Top 5 countries in the Caribbean influenced By Africa 55

XIII.   **Moses & Israel** 63

XIV.   The list of religious concepts originating in Africa..................69

XV.   Africa and the Bible: 73

XVI.	The List of Famous Biblical Persons
Associated with Africa 75

XVII.	Interesting Facts about Africa and Israel
not in the Bible 79

XVIII.	The List of Famous Biblical Lands Inhabited
by Black Africans (Palestine) 81

XIX.	**Coltrane & The United States of America**................87

XX.	The List of Western Music Forms Derived from Africa.........93

XXI.	The Brief List of European Instruments
Brought to the West by Africans 95

XXII.	The List of Dance Forms Created
by Persons of African Descent.......................................97

XXIII.	The List of Cities Where Jazz Originated...................99

XXIV.	The List of Six World Class Artists of African Descent........101

XXV.	John Coltrane and his influence on
American music and culture 105

XXVI.	The List of Great American Jazz Composers
and Performers of African Descent..............................109

XXVII.	Summary 123

XXVIII.	African Art Essay 127

XXIX.	My core beliefs 131

XXX.	ISAIAH 19:19-21...133

XXXI.	About the Author..135

I

Introduction

While visiting the Caribbean, North Africa, South America, Southern Europe and the Middle East, I noticed a commonality of features and characteristics throughout those geographical regions. The common thread that I found in each area was some type of African cultural influence readily visible in one aspect or another in the society. Since I went to different regions of the world with the intent of finding African influences in various aspects of the cultures I visited, I was both excited and pleasantly surprised to find out how extensive this influence has been.

I learned of monuments and parks named after famous Black Americans. I observed firsthand major cultural influences in a wide variety of ways - I saw palaces built by North African Blacks in Spain, variations of African drum music in Brasil, African familial classification systems used in Israeli history books, and mosaic patterns carved onto the boardwalks of Rio De Janeiro's beaches, symbolizing the African, European and South American Indian racial unity and harmony of the society.

I also read about North African artistic influences on mosaic patterns discovered among the ruins of several Greek islands and studied striking sculptured figures created in Jamaica and Haiti which signify their strong identification with their African heritage and roots.

While looking for examples of how Africa has influenced other cultures, Spain really became an impetus for my travelling to other parts of the world, looking for more examples of this African influence. While on a ferry bringing me from Morocco back to the Costa Del Sol of Spain, a group of South American tourists on the ferry began singing and clapping their hands in rhythms that had a strong percussive sound and whose rhythmic variations sounded West African in nature. I asked another tourist where these people were from and I was told Brazil. Upon returning to the States, I began listening to Brazilian music and reading about Brazilian culture and found out that this country is connected to Africa in many artistic, aesthetic, and spiritual ways. This gave me an even stronger desire to make a firsthand investigation of this and other geographic regions of the world to find their connection to the motherland; a connection that is not often discussed in this or other western cultures.

Thus, my trip to Spain was a revealing experience for me, as much for what I saw going to and from the country (as in seeing brown skinned Moroccans in Morocco) as for what I saw in Spain itself. This included architectural ruins, music and a history that is undeniably connected to Africa, while not admitted openly by historians or everyday citizens.

The purpose of the book is to point out those influences to the reader, and while doing so assist the reader in redefining what is normally considered or accepted in this culture as being contributions to civilization made by those of African descent.

The uncommon and unique signs of African influence on the 'other continents,' the architectural, musical, religious, racial, legal, artistic, linguistic and historical influences that I will discuss in this book represent and are the result of a lifetime of my experiences.

Africa's influence on world herstory/history/ourstory (to coin a phrase used by publisher Jacquetta Parhams), has been vast, immeasurable and magnanimous. Join me as I take a journey to search for a greater understanding of my relationship with the continent that gave birth to the homo sapien species and gave birth to civilization on this planet.

II

The Process

One of the reasons I wrote this book is that I feel not enough books are being written by Afrocentric scholars that give general information on various geographical regions of the world to examine their cultural and spiritual relationship to Africa. There are many books being written about Kemite and its connection to Black Africa, and there will always be a range of books written about the achievements of African Americans and ancient African cultures.

But not enough research is being done (or at least published) on the complexities and intricate details of African influences on western cultures. Van Sertima has been one of the most successful authors in getting this information to the general public, and he and Dr. Charles Finch and Dr. Ben Yohanan pick up where the great scholars of old such as Dr. Diop have left off.

For example, more information needs to be published in the field of Afrocentricity on the myth of oral traditions being "primitive" as is discussed briefly in the myths section of this book. Also, Afrocentric scholars need to publish more information on the Nubian culture, Sub Saharan African civilizations, and the high level of sophistication of those societies.

This book does (as other books of this nature) draw upon the vast information compiled by scholars who came before us to document the Nubian culture and its achievements. It traces for the reader how ancient African cultures such as Nubia influenced other African cultures such as ancient Kemite, which then had a profound impact on ancient Greece and the development of modern western societies.

In the process of doing all this, it should become clear to the reader how and why it is possible that entire regions of the world - the Caribbean, Southern Europe and South America in particular, can be redefined and reclassified as being a part of Africa.

Therefore, this book is not a dissertation on African history nor, does it dwell on any one particular subject matter pertaining to the more than 200 cultural groups who inhabit the motherland. Nor is it merely a compilation of facts about Afro-American history and the influence of the Black American on the cultural and industrial development of American society, though it contains information about that influence.

The premise of this book is that the people of Africa played and continue to play a central role in the history of the world.

The purpose of this book is to examine this central role that Africa played from an aesthetic perspective and point out details on many achievements that we commonly think of as European, actually originated in Africa.

This book seeks to educate the reader by presenting information about the motherland by providing a list of people, places and concepts that have been classified as having originated in western culture and reclassifying them as having come from the motherland.

This book is about re-ordering one's worldview about all things African so that when the reader is finished, he or she, as an American or a person of color, will have a greater understanding of the interdependence of Western and African cultures throughout herstory/history. While reading this book, it should become clear that a process is taking place here, one which lists the scientific, scholarly and cultural contributions made by Black Africans both in Africa and throughout the world. Near the end of the book, I also give concrete examples of how western scholars have categorized African achievements in such a manner as to diminish, or in some instances, erase any evidence indicating that those contributions were made by Black Africans. This was done to perpetuate the myth that the most extraordinary steps taken to further advance human progress were initiated by southern European civilizations.

By assisting the reader in observing and appreciating the African influence on the development of Western and world history, this book should aid the reader in their quest for self-actualization, as he or she seeks to understand and be proud of his or her own heritage, whatever it may be; but particularly if that person is of African descent.

III

Who's Black and Who's Not

Throughout this book, African cultural groups and individuals are discussed who have made significant, interesting, and astounding contributions to the development of African and Western societies. Until recently, many of the African cultural groups and individuals discussed in this work have been classified as non-Black by Euro centric writers.

Many scholars are now in the process of confirming and rediscovering research done earlier in this century by historians such as Diop and W.E.B. Dubois. Those two legendary scholars and others wrote extensively about ancient Egyptians and the Moors and their racial and historical connection to equatorial Africa. When a cultural group is discussed where some disagreement exists concerning their racial origin, I will explain and justify my point of view.

In dealing with a discussion of who's Black and who's not, it should be fairly obvious that individuals who possess medium or dark brown skin, shorter and more narrow bridges above their noses, fully formed and prominent lips and other Negroid features are considered of Black African descent, even if they have mixed with another racial group sometime in their history. It is illogical to say that an African group is not Black simply because they have intermarried or intermingled with another racial group since genetically speaking, where one parent is Black and the other is not, African genes tend to dominate.

Any offspring of a Black and non-Black union usually tend to resemble the Black parent more than the non-Black parent, and in some cases the non-Black parent's racial influence is barely noticeable.

While discussing how America has and continues to perceive race, let's take a look at an international research project that focuses on race and genetic variation. This research project will help further our understanding of how race has been used in the US and other Western countries to validate their view of how separate we are as humans. This view is opposite to what is now being accepted by most genetic researchers, having the understanding that most of the variations within the genetic family we know as Homo Sapiens are social constructs.

The Human Genome Project (HGP) is an example of how race is viewed as a socio-political construct in several ways. The HGP was an international scientific research effort that aimed to map and sequence the entire human genome, which was completed in 2003. While the HGP focused on understanding the genetic basis of human traits and diseases, it also shed light on the concept of race and its complexities.

When looking at genetic variation and race, the HGP demonstrated that human genetic variation is continuous and gradual rather than discrete and categorical. In other words, there is more genetic variation within racial or ethnic groups than between them. This finding challenges the notion that there are distinct and genetically homogenous racial groups, which in my view indicates that race is not a well-defined biological concept, but rather a (complex) social construct. It has been agreed upon by a number of Afro-centric scholars that race is a social construct.

The concept of race is a product of historical, cultural, and socio-political factors rather than a highly-defined genetic reality. Different societies throughout history have categorized people into racial groups based on physical characteristics, geography, cultural practices, and so forth. These categories have often been used to justify social slavery, hierarchies based on skin color, discrimination, and unequal access to resources and opportunities here in the US, and in other regions of the world that have used the concept of race to oppress another group of people. The HGP's findings reinforce the notion that race does not have a meaningful biological origin. It highlights the fact that genetic differences between persons or groups of people are not significant enough to warrant the classification of humans into distinct races, as there is more genetic diversity within racial groups than between them.

It is interesting that in the US, race is defined in a unique way and differs from how it is viewed in other parts of the world. The US has a long history of slavery, segregation, and discrimination, which has deeply influenced the country's understanding of race and identity. For example, in the US, race has historically been based on visible physical traits, such as skin color, and individuals have been classified into distinct racial categories (e.g., White, Black, Asian, Native American). However, this system of classification does not reflect the complexity of human genetic variation, and ignores the significant genetic diversity within each racial group in the US. In fact, some Americans seem to be unaware of the diversity within communities of color including religious and linguistic differences that take place within the Black community, for one example.

Other parts of the world may have different approaches to categorizing and defining race, often based on local histories, cultural backgrounds, and regional demographics. Some countries use differences in ethnic, tribal, or national identities as a means of fostering a sense of culture and belonging instead of the specific racial categories commonly used in the US. Therefore, the Human Genome Project's findings support the notion and/or perspective that race is a socio-political construct rather, than a genetic entity that can be identified by racial categories. The genetic variation within and between racial groups, as revealed by the HGP, challenges the notion of discrete racial categories. The US has a unique history and approach to defining race that has played a significant role in shaping how race is understood in this country, and is used to discriminate against communities of color in the US, and to view those groups as inferior in some ways or fashion.

In the past as well as in the present, when certain African groups such as the Kemites (Egyptians) have made extraordinary contributions to the history of the world, questions arise as to the racial heritage of the tribe. But one point must be made clear; all African tribes described in this book come from ancestors who are genetically linked to equatorial Africa. These groups possess the same racial features, share a common history and heritage, and share common ancestors with the Black African groups surrounding them, as well as identify themselves as being African peoples of color.

Accordingly, some critics would say that it was a mixture of Arabs or Berbers with some of the African tribes such as the Moors that made them great, but my response would be the opposite; the

African blood in tribes such as the Moors made them great since their ancestors have considerable experience in greatness. The Blackness of many African civilizations has caused them to make prolific, creative, and spectacular contributions to this planet's history. Millennium after millennium, century after century. Africa has given our planet one of the world's first continuous governments led by a constitutional monarchy, as well as several of the world's earliest dynasties.

IV

The List of 10 most Prevalent Myths About Africa

I've known rivers:

I've known rivers ancient as the world and older than the flow of human blood in human veins.

My soul has grown deep like the rivers.

I bathed in the Euphrates when dawns were young.

I built my hut near the Congo and it lulled me to sleep.

I looked upon the Nile and raised the pyramids above it.

I heard the singing of the Mississippi when Abe Lincoln went down to New Orleans, and I've seen its muddy bosom turn

all golden in the Sunset.

I've known rivers:

Ancient dusky rivers.

My soul has grown deep like the rivers.

" The Negro Speaks of Rivers" by Langston Hughes

1. Civilization began in what is now present-day Greece:

    The first evidence of continuous civilization was found in East Africa thousands of years before ancient Greece became organized into city-states. The ancient Nubians (Ethiopians) preceded the Kemites and both the Nubian and the Ancient Kemites were thriving thousands of years before Greek civilization began.

2. Black Africans do not have a continuous ancient history:

    The opposite is true. Africans who belong to tribes that can trace their heritage to equatorial Africa have the longest most continuous history of any cultural/tribal group on earth. This is because of their connection to the Egyptian and Ethiopian cultures, both of which are descendants of the Nubians, the earliest inhabitants of East Africa near present day Kenya. North East Africa gave the world language, tool technology, the world's first and oldest continuous universities still in existence, and the first organized belief in one G-d, (monotheism).

3. African cultures are more primitive than Western and Asian cultures because oral traditions, found especially in West Africa, are a more primitive means of communication and

    storing information than written traditions:

    Here are some facts that should clarify this matter; the earliest alphabet used by Western cultures was developed by the Phoenicians, an Afro-Asiatic people who were colonized by the ancient Kemites (Egyptians); Most tribes in West Africa and/or villages that use oral tradition as a means of storing cultural history have a Griot (historian) who has the responsibility of collecting the patrilineal and matrilineal ancestry of the tribe and recording and memorizing all important events taking place in the last several hundred years for that tribe; keep in mind that the familial lineage systems in many West African societies are so complicated that Western anthropologists in the past have used calculus to comprehend the relationships between relatives; the earliest known written symbols of communication - pictographic script (hieroglyphics) was created by the Kemitic tribe and it should be noted that African written symbols precede all European written traditions; Black American scholars have recently noticed that oral tradition-based African tribes as may be found in Ghana often have complex patterns carved into their artwork; these geometric designs use visual cues as a means of telling key aspects of the culture's history. The information discussed above is evidence of written symbols being used in an area of Africa that supposedly has no written traditions.

4. The continent of Africa is mostly composed of jungles:

Africa has the largest desert in the world in terms of square miles (see section on the geography of Africa). Africa is largely composed of forests, plains, and deserts. It is interesting to note that the continent of South America has the largest rainforest or jungle in the world, located in Brasil (the Amazon).

5. Christianity began in Europe:

The first organized church established by a group of non-Jewish followers of Christ outside of ancient Israel was in Kemite (Egypt) and was later called the Coptic Church. The Coptic Church was established in the first century of the Common Era (or AD, After Christ) according to the Bible Almanac and it continues to exist as it has for almost two millennia in Kemite, Ethiopia, and other countries in northern Africa. It is an accepted fact by most Western and African scholars that the Coptic Church predates the Catholic Church (established in the 3rd century, C.E.) by almost 200 hundred years. (See section on Religions Originating in Africa).

6. Judaism as a religion began in Asia:

Well, yes and no. Since Abraham is seen as the progenitor or father of the Jewish people and was born in the Middle East, it is historically correct to say that Jewish culture began in Asia with him. However, it is also correct to state that the religion of Judaism began in Africa since Moses according to the Bible was born and raised in Kemite (Egypt), and the 12 tribes had lived in Africa for 400 years before their G-d chose to whisper into Moses' ear the Torah (Law), and reveal to the Jews their destiny as being the Griots or custodians of G-d's word.

7. Ancient Kemite (Egypt) was inhabited primarily by Arabs who were white (of European/Asian descent):

In examining the racial background of the Arabs, one should note that according to the Bible, Arabs are descendants of Esau, the son of Ishmael, who himself was the son of Abraham and his Black African concubine. According to African American scholars, African historians, and the Bible, Arabs did not wander into North Africa in great numbers until the advent of Islam, approximately 1300 years ago. Ancient Kemite was originally inhabited by a race of brown-skinned people who originated in what the ancient Egyptians called the upper Nile, and is now known as Ethiopia according to an article in Time magazine on the African influence on Greek civilization on 9-23-91.

8. North Africa is inhabited by Berbers, Arabs, and Moors, cultural groups who are descendants of Caucasian peoples:

    It is true that the Berbers, a tribe of Eurasian heritage, settled in Africa long before the Arabs wandered into North Africa. But it is also true that the Moorish tribes, who were separate and distinct from the Arabs and Berbers, are one of the original tribes inhabiting northern Africa, and have been there for thousands of years (see section on the Moors).

9. East Africans such as the Ethiopians are descendants of the Semite tribes from the Middle East and are therefore Caucasian:

    This myth is part of a conscious effort by Western scholars to ensure that history books do not indicate that the beginning of civilization began in Black Africa. Since most scholars agree that the first evidence of civilization as well as the first evidence of homo sapien life is found in East Africa, western historians had no choice but to attempt to reclassify the racial heritage of the tribal groups inhabiting that area of Africa. But according to an article in the Washington Post on 1-13-87, which discusses the search for the first homo sapien by University of California scientists engaged in genetic studies of evolutionary relationships, all fully modern homo sapiens are descendants of a group of females who inhabited East Africa. This African population became the ancestors of the ancient Nubians.

    The understanding that Homo sapiens originated in Africa is based on an extensive amount of anthropological and genetic studies. The hypothesis, known as the "Out of Africa" or "African Replacement" theory, presents the notion that modern humans, Homo sapiens, evolved in Africa and then migrated and replaced earlier hominin populations, and migrated to other parts of the world.

Here are some key points and primary anthropological sources that support this theory:

Mitochondrial Eve: This is one of the more significant ideas that came out of anthropological research called Mitochondrial DNA studies. This research presents well-supported idea that all living humans today share a common female ancestor, often referred to as "Mitochondrial Eve." This ancestral woman is thought to have lived in Africa around 150,000 to 200,000 years ago, supporting the African origin of our species.

Archaeological Evidence: Archaeological sites in Africa have provided evidence of early human behaviors, cultural practices, and technological advancements that are consistent with the development of modern human traits.

For primary anthropological sources that investigate the "Out of Africa" theory and Homo sapiens' origin in Africa, you can refer to research papers published in scientific journals such as "Nature," "Science," "Proceedings of the National Academy of Sciences," and "Journal of Human Evolution." Also, works by well-known and respected anthropologists in the field, such as Chris Stringer, Richard Leakey, and Svante Pääbo, also explore the topic of the African origin of the Homa Sapien species in detail.

African Eve During their 8000-year tenure in Africa, the Nubians absorbed or mixed with various other racial groups who wandered in and out of Africa throughout history such as the Greeks, the Assyrians, and the ancient Israelites etc. But to say that the Nubians are descendants of Caucasians is illogical since there is currently no verifiable data in existence to validate that theory. It would be similar to saying that all Latin peoples are Black just because they mixed with the Moors in Southern Europe and mixed with West Africans in South America, or that African-Americans are of Caucasian descent simply because the majority of Black Americans have some white ancestors in their family tree.

10. Africa is a poor continent with few resources and a scarcity of material wealth:

Here is a list of some African countries that are considered to have successful economies as of 2021:

1. Ethiopia: One of the fastest-growing economies in Africa, Ethiopia has been experiencing strong GDP growth, driven by sectors such as agriculture, manufacturing, and services.

2. Rwanda: Rwanda's economy has been growing steadily due to infrastructure development and business-friendly policies, and has a focus on technology and innovation.

3. Ghana: Ghana has done well in recent years, showing growth in the areas of agriculture, mining, oil, and services.

4. Ivory Coast (Côte d'Ivoire): This West African nation has experienced significant and rapid economic growth, in the areas of agriculture, energy, and manufacturing.

5. Kenya: Kenya is a leading economy in East Africa, with a strong focus on technology, telecommunications, and financial services.

6. Tanzania: Tanzania's economy has been growing steadily, supported by an increase in agriculture, mining, tourism, and telecommunications.

7. Senegal has a stable political environment, and this West African country's economy has been expanding, with investments in infrastructure, energy, and services.

8. Botswana: Botswana has a well-managed economy, and a stable democratic government driven by the diamond industry and sound economic policies. The government is currently working

on diversifying its economy to have less reliance on mining ore, nickel, and other precious metals so that it can continue to be self-sustaining and more reliant on the emergence of new technologies.

9. Mauritius is known for its stable economy and favorable business environment, and has a strong focus on financial services, tourism, and manufacturing.

10. Egypt: As one of the largest economies in Africa, this ancient country's growth has been driven by manufacturing, construction, and tourism services.

In Western and Southern Africa, many countries (such as South Africa) are mineral rich, but until they became free from European colonialization, they were unable to benefit from or compete with Western nations in an open market economy. Up until twenty to thirty years ago, the British and other European colonialist powers had maintained corporations in Africa whose purpose was to export and exploit the natural resources of each country (copper, uranium, rubber, diamonds etc.) and sell it to whatever country had ordered it for manufacturing purposes. This, in effect, means that the countries where the minerals were taken from did not benefit from the exportation of their material goods. Also, a huge labor drain took place in West Africa during the slave trade years (1600-1800's). The creation of the slave market in the Americas as well as the conquering of West African tribes by other West African tribes _and_ European colonialists reduced or in some instances destroyed the geopolitical and cultural infrastructures existing in those societies. Walter Rodney discussed extensively in his book "How Europe Underdeveloped Africa" how a combination of power politics and economic exploitation of Africa by Europeans led to the poor state of African political and economic development evident in the late 20th century.

Slavery interfered with many West African tribes' economic, social, and technological development. Also, the creation of artificial borders in West Africa by the colonialist powers without regard for the former tribal boundaries which had been in existence for thousands of years, caused tension to arise between various African tribes. But while discussing the material wealth (or lack of) in Africa, let us briefly examine some Western European countries such as France and Britain which are doing well economically even though their countries were in a state of chaos and economic devastation at the end of WWII. One may ask how those countries recuperated so quickly. Is it that France and Britain have some innate ability to survive and emerge from disasters that African countries lack? I should think not. In the book How NATO Weakens the West, the author states that 40% of our defense budget in the mid-1980s went to support NATO. Over the years Western Europe has been heavily subsidized by the United States for years as a buffer zone to the communist countries they border such as the now former U.S.S.R. The article states that "by paying 134 billion dollars last year (in 1985) to NATO Alliance countries we are turning them into welfare states. By maintaining NATO we are making our allies weaker and weaker and more dependent on U.S. military presence and financial support." Also, while discussing the supposed lack of resources found in Africa, let us not forget The relationship between terrorism, oil, and US engagement in the Middle East and how those concerns on a very contemporary level have had significant implications for the West, and have served to weaken America and drained her economic and military resources. It's important to note that this is a highly nuanced and evolving topic that requires a comprehensive understanding of historical and geopolitical factors. Here are some key points to consider:

1. Terrorism and its impact on the West: Terrorist attacks carried out by extremist groups, particularly those with a jihadist

ideology, have targeted Western countries and citizens. These attacks have caused significant human suffering and loss of life, as well as psychological and economic impacts, creating fear and uncertainty. In response, Western nations have been compelled to devote substantial resources to counterterrorism efforts, both domestically and internationally.

Some of the negative effects of terrorism on the West include:

Economic costs: The cost of combating terrorism, fortifying security measures, and dealing with the aftermath of attacks can place a strain on national budgets and impact economic growth.

Oil and its impact on the West: The Middle East has been a crucial region for oil production, with some of the world's largest oil reserves located there. The West, particularly the United States, has been heavily reliant on Middle Eastern oil to meet its energy demands. This dependence has influenced Western countries' foreign policies, sometimes leading to strategic alliances with oil-rich Middle Eastern nations.

a. Vulnerability to oil shocks: Reliance on Middle Eastern oil has made Western economies vulnerable to fluctuations in oil prices, geopolitical tensions, and supply disruptions, affecting energy prices and overall economic stability.

b. Geopolitical entanglements: To protect their oil interests, Western countries have at times engaged in complex relationships with Middle Eastern governments, which can be politically challenging and may lead to unintended consequences.

2. US engagement in the Middle East: The United States has played a significant role in the Middle East, particularly since the end of World War II. US involvement in the region has been driven by

various factors, including the desire to ensure stability, protect its allies, access to oil, and counterterrorism efforts.

a. Military interventions: US military engagements in the Middle East, such as the wars in Iraq and Afghanistan, have resulted in significant financial costs, and those wars have sometimes faced criticism for being lengthy and inconclusive.

b. Strain on international relations: US actions in the region have often strained relations, caused tension with allies, and raised concerns about the exercise of American power and heightened the fear of America being and Imperial Power.

Additionally, the difference between many so-called third-world African countries and many so-called technologically advanced Western countries lies in the amount of money, which in this case is billions of American tax dollars, that continues to pour into those countries' economies each year in spite of the fact that the cold war is over. Until the U.S.S.R. disintegrated recently, those subsidies were used not only to protect America and Europe from communism, but also to protect the image the U.S. Government has created of Europe as a region of the world that is superior, invincible, and capable of sustaining itself no matter how many disasters it faces.

V

THE TOP 4 COUNTRIES OF THE WORLD INFLUENCED BY AFRICA

The following is a list of criteria used to decide if a country or culture is historically connected to Africa:

- Religion
- Education
- Philosophy
- Architecture
- Science
- Medicine
- Law
- History

- Racial Heritage
- Literature
- Language
- Cultural commonalities

In order to be included in the next section of the book, Africa must have had a major impact on the countries listed - enough to influence the history of the people or affect the daily rituals of the culture. If one regards various European countries as having made a profound effect on various countries in Africa because they colonized parts of Africa, then consider this: African

exploration of Europe preceded European colonization of Africa by

some several thousand years.

Realizing this, it becomes easy to discuss or note African influence on Western cultures that were colonized, conquered, or otherwise explored by Africans who are genetically linked to equatorial Africa. Similarly, countries heavily populated by Black slaves in the Western hemisphere are also noted as being heavily influenced by African cultures since these slaves lived in the Americas, and had a profound effect on the cultures and the lands they inhabited. Here is the list of continents and countries of the world - African in nature:

VI

Spain

Herstory:

Of all the countries in Europe, Spain probably has the longest and most continuous history of cultural ties with Africa. Strategically located at the mouth of the Mediterranean, the rock of Gibraltar has been used as an entry point for various African groups to reach the Iberian Peninsula and for various Euro-Asian groups to enter Africa for over 2000 years. Science: Moors from Northern Africa made various scientific, technological, mathematical, and agricultural contributions to Spain that would enable that culture to become civilized. Not only did the various Moorish tribes' rule of Spain cause that society to advance and become a more complex society, but it also ushered in an age of enlightenment for other groups such as the Spanish Jews who lived in Spain during the era of Moorish occupation. During Moorish rule, Jewish culture blossomed. Jewish philosophy developed to new heights and some of the most famous of all Jewish writers and interpreters of Jewish Rabbinic law lived during that period. In fact, when the Moors were finally expelled from Spain, Jewish Philosophers such as Maimonides, perhaps the greatest of all modern Jewish scholars in Europe, decided to return to Africa.

Why did Jewish culture blossom during Moorish rule? It occurred for several reasons: Religion

1. Religion: Spain was a Catholic country that was at that time experiencing animosity towards the Jews because the Jews (they believed) did not believe in their own Messiah. This anti-Semitism also caused internal conflicts for Catholic leaders since they continually harassed their Jewish citizens while worshipping a son of G-d born of a Jewish woman. The Moors did not harbor such extreme animosity towards the Jewish people.

2. Spanish culture is not as ancient as Jewish culture - the Spanish had animosity towards a people who possessed a heritage that predates theirs by several thousand years. Yet the Jewish people shared an ancient past with their Moorish conquerors and flourished under Moorish rule probably because they shared similar religious beliefs, and both have had a long tradition of academic excellence dating back thousands of years.

Spain: Of all the countries in Europe, Spain is probably the one place where an individual student of history could say that the history of that civilization is also the history of Africa. As it is discussed in the book, Spanish herstory/history is clearly connected to Africa from a geographic perspective due to the close proximity of Spain and Portugal making up what is called the Iberian Peninsula If Africa begins at the Pyrenees, as was declared by a 17th century French cardinal, it is because its geographic location is a crossroads of the world. Spain is especially a crossroads between Africa and Euro-Asia, the Atlantic and the Mediterranean, Christianity, Islam and Judaism, the old and the new. It was, 1000 years ago, a place where the scientific achievements and educational emphasis of North African civilizations would first be brought to European civilizations, and a place where Asian immigrant groups such as the Jews from Palestine would find a brief refuge from Catholic oppression. Racial heritage; The racial mixing produced over a period of time, would produce a new race of people called Latinos who would then go to South America and the Caribbean and mix again with people of African and Native/Indigenous South American and Caribbean descent, and produce the various cultural groups called the: Hispanic/Latino ethnic groups. Many Spanish ruins, which comprise some of the oldest educational and religious institutions and buildings still in existence in Europe, were conceived of and built by Africans. Its musical, religious, and linguistic characteristics all have traces of Africa still visible to this day. This book discusses how The Moors' historical origins can be traced back to the Arab-Berber Muslim conquest of North Africa in the 7th and 8th centuries. Arab armies led by Umayyad Caliphate generals, such as Tariq ibn Ziyad, crossed from North Africa to the Iberian Peninsula in 711 CE, beginning the process of Islamic rule in Spain.

Most Western and European scholars agree that Spain and other countries were colonized/conquered/explored by persons from Northern Africa. Furthermore, most Western scholars would hesitantly agree that the Moors are native to Africa and that this tribe had a profound influence on the cultural development of several countries in Southern Europe. The part of this discussion that most white scholars find difficult to accept, and is the most controversial, is the notion that the Moors who colonized Spain and other countries in So. Europe are native Africans, who did not mix with Southern Europeans and do not have a significant amount of white genes in them. There is no agreement among white, European, African American, and African scholars as to the racial features and genetic origin of the tribe. The next section of this chapter will address this issue.

Most Western historians believe that the Moors are composed of any tribe found in North Africa, of Asian or Arab descent, who wandered into or conquered parts of Europe. However, when one examines the features of the statues of Moorish soldiers still standing in Moorish Castles, or observes the racial mixtures of the inhabitants still in Morocco and in Spain, it is evident that members of the tribes categorized as Moors who came into Southern Europe were descendants of people from equatorial Africa.

1. In the book Iberia by James Michener, one picture shows a Moor with Pigmy-like facial features, visual proof of the genetic connection to equatorial Africa of many of those who came to Europe. "Muslim Spain and Portugal: A Political History of Al-Andalus" by Hugh Kennedy - provides a comprehensive review of the history of Muslim Spain, including the Moors' rule over Spain and their interactions with other cultures in the region.

2. "A History of Islamic Spain" by W. Montgomery Watt explores the political, social, and cultural aspects of Islamic Spain, providing insights into the Moors' influence on the Iberian Peninsula.

The Moors are indigenous to Northwest Africa, conquered Southern Europe, and explored and traveled to Northern and Eastern Europe twice in history. The last time they visited Europe was over a thousand years ago. They can still be found in present-day Morocco and Spain.

Carthaginians - This ancient tribe is an ancestor to the Moorish tribe, and lived in Northwest to Northcentral Africa near present-day Tunisia. Hannibal is a descendant of that tribe and he and his military units crossed over the Strait of Gibraltar in a military campaign in which they came close to conquering the entire Roman.

VII

The Moors

The Black African Tribe that Africanized Spain

Once upon a time, there was a tribe that inhabited northwest and north central Africa. This tribe, later called the Iberios tribe (since they settled later into the Iberian Peninsula) is also known as the Moors, who were to become some of the most famous explorers in antiquity.

The Moors, who were predominantly Muslims of North African and of North African descent, played a significant role in helping develop various aspects of European societies during their presence in Europe. The Moors' influence on Europe can be traced primarily to their rule in the Iberian Peninsula (modern-day Spain and Portugal) as well as their time colonizing and exploring other parts of the Mediterranean and Southern Europe during the Middle Ages.

1. **Al-Andalus and Islamic Spain**: One of the most notable contributions of the Moors was their establishment of the Umayyad Caliphate of Cordoba in 929 CE, creating Al-Andalus, a prosperous Muslim kingdom in the Iberian Peninsula. Al-Andalus was a center of learning, culture, and art. Scholars, scientists, and philosophers made significant advancements in various fields, including mathematics, astronomy, medicine, and literature which had a lasting influence on the development of scholarly learning in Spain and Portugal. Many Greek and Roman texts that had been lost in the rest of Europe were preserved and translated in Al-Andalus by the Moors, and eventually made their way back to Europe through later translations.

2. **Architecture and Urban Planning**: The Moors brought an advanced knowledge of architecture and urban planning. The architectural structures they built in Spain are legendary. The Moors introduced innovative building techniques, such as the use of arches, domes, and intricate tilework, which are indicative of the influence of African and Muslim architectural styles they brought with them from Africa. The African influence left a lasting impact on the architectural style of Europe. The influence of Moorish architecture can be seen in stunning palaces and iconic landmarks such as the Alhambra in Granada, Spain, and the Great Mosque of Córdoba.

It's important to note that the Moors were eventually expelled from Spain in 1492, and their influence declined over time as Europe experienced its own cultural and intellectual developments. Nonetheless, their historical impact on European societies, particularly in the Iberian Peninsula, remains significant and is recognized as a crucial period of cultural exchange and development in Europe's herstory/history.

Most instruments of the symphony orchestra have an Afro-Asiatic origin and were brought to Europe by the Moors and Arabs, and can be traced to North Africa and the Near East. The lute is an instrument brought to Britain by the Romans and was probably given to them by explorers from North Africa.

The Bagpipe, according to the book Music and World Culture is an African instrument, the largest of which is found in Egypt. It was carried up to Scotland probably by Moors, Arabs, and/or Romans.

The Moors conquered the peninsula south of the Pyrenees as well as other parts of southern Europe, including Portugal, France, Italy, and Greece. They left a technological, religious, agricultural, educational, and architectural influence that lasted up to the present millennium of the Common Era.

As has been mentioned before, western historians have cited these people as being of mixed Berber and Arab descent. Some encyclopedias blatantly write that they are white. For example, the 1987 edition of World Book states "A common but incorrect belief that Moors are Negroes was spread by William Shakespeare's play 'Othello.' Moors belong to the Mediterranean group of the Caucasoid (white) race" This attitude is prevalent among Western scholars. It is easier to explain the vast cultural contributions obtained by the Southern European cultures if their colonizers are white Africans rather than native Africans who are direct descendants of a tribe from the equatorial regions of Africa.

Even though the Moors remain a controversy with some unenlightened scholars, several points can be made to verify their direct connection to equatorial Africa:

1. They portrayed themselves in many instances as having what Westerners would call West African, and in some instances

pygmy-like features when depicting themselves in statues (they used a naturalistic style of art that did not obscure features for artistic purposes). This is evidence of a true representation of their physical features. (See page 549 in the Book <u>Iberia</u> for example).

2. When traveling to Morocco, Moors are still visible and are visibly distinct from Arabs with brown to dark brown skin and African and/or Negroid features.

3. Arabs, Berbers, and other groups who were not the original inhabitants of North Africa wandered into Africa during the last 1500 years. Many of these tribes came to Europe during the same time the more African Moors were conquering and exploring that geographic region, and brought the religion of Islam with them. These groups were also called Moors, and consisted of several distinct tribes of Berbers, as well as various Arab tribes. These tribes came as distinct cultural groups and were not considered the only tribes to come from Northern Africa to Spain and Europe, although European historians frequently mislabeled Arabs and Berbers as Moors, further confusing the picture historically. As explained in the beginning of the book, where I used a quote from the Washington Post describing who will be considered African, if a person has West or Central African physical characteristics, they will be considered of that heritage in this book. To say that some Moorish tribes that originated in Africa have physical characteristics similar to persons who inhabit West or Central Africa, but are white only because they were responsible for significant cultural advancements of Southern European civilizations is ludicrous. Accordingly, if white scientists want to say that all North and East African tribes such as the Ethiopians, Moors, Sudanese, and Egyptians are either mixed or white because they have mixed with Asian (Semitic) or Euro-Asian (Berber or Mediterranean groups) and have dolichocephalic head

shapes, one must use the same rationale when discussing other minority groups. White scientists must say, for example, that Afro-Americans and Afro-Brazilians who are brown-skinned and have black physical characteristics, are also white since they as a group have mixed much more recently and in larger numbers with whites in the new world than ancient Africans did. However, American scientists would be unwilling to say this since it would disrupt the entire race/class system that is a basic part of the economic and social infrastructure in this country. Also, African Americans are proud to be a part of their great African heritage, and do not want to be considered white.

VIII

The Moors 'list' of Achievements

- Built the Alhambra Palace in Spain, one of the most architecturally splendid structures in the world - built in the 9th century of the Common Era. "The Alhambra" by Robert Irwin.

- Explored or conquered Spain, Portugal, France, and the ancient Roman empire twice in history (the first time the Roman empire was invaded was during the time of Hannibal; the second time was 1000 years ago). They also explored Greece, Britain, Ireland, and Russia. In the book "Black Africans in Renaissance Europe" by T. F. Earle and K. J. P. Lowe, the authors explore the presence of Africans, including Moors, in various parts of Europe during the Renaissance period.

- Influenced the architectural design of structures such as the

- Brought Islam to Spain and Europe.

- During Moorish rule in Spain, as incredible Jewish philosophical and cultural advancements took place. Many great Jewish philosophers flourished during this period of history.

- Spanish medical, technological, agricultural, and architectural advancements took place during Moorish rule in Spain as well as in other countries nearby such as Portugal.

- The influence of the Moors was so strong and long-lasting that operas written by Italian composers still portray the Moors as a regal people. Othello, perhaps one of the world's most elegant operas is an epic tale of a Moor who remained in Italy after the period of Moorish domination was over. An officer in the Venetian navy, Othello had conflicts over living in a foreign land once occupied and colonized by his people. The opera called Othello was written by Giuseppe Verdi and was adapted from the famous play of the same name by Shakespeare.

- Moorish influence can be felt as far north as Britain. When the Moors were explorers, they went as far as northern Europe in exploration and conquest (see section on Britain page).

- It is safe to say that the development of Southern European civilization (as it occurred after 1000 C.E.) would not have taken place had the Moors not conquered Europe. They carried musical instruments with them to Europe and greatly influenced the development of Western music notations by carrying those art forms from the Middle East to Europe.

IX

Top 4 countries in Europe influenced by Africa

Spain is not the only country in Southern Europe to be heavily influenced by Northern African/Moors, or even more ancient African tribes such as the Nubian and Kemites.

Let's examine:

Greece - In the book Black Athena, The Afro-Asiatic Roots of Classical Civilization, Mr. Martin Barnal discusses what was until recently discarded information by European historians concerning the colonialization of ancient Greece by ancient (pre-Arab) Egypt. Mr. Barnal's work is an excellent scholarship model to study and use for research. Yet one does not need to read this book to find evidence of the ancient Egyptian and Nubian empires as having been major influences on Greek and Middle Eastern societies. Egyptian civilization is mentioned in the Bible as having existed long before many other non African cultures; and again Egyptian culture precedes Greek culture by some 2000 years. But in light of the evidence presented in Mr. Bernal's book, evidence which discusses great advances made by Greek civilization after having been colonized by the culturally sophisticated Egyptians, his book lists the scientific, medical, philosophical, and technological advances made by the Greeks as being a consequence of African colonialization.

Since Greek civilization is viewed by Western scientists as the beginning of western civilization, this in effect sets the stage for scholars/educators making the statement that European civilization could not have advanced to its present state were it not for the influence on it by ancient African societies such as Nubia and Kemite. Also, the library at Alexandria (an ancient African city) was used by the Greeks to house/store their gathered knowledge. But the question becomes why use an African city? The answer is that it was known for its written treasures and it would therefore be more appropriate to put a library there than anywhere in the Western world. The Greeks conquered and interacted with various people of African ancestry in North Africa. Throughout history, they fought wars against various African tribes who were not as successful in conquering them as the ancient Egyptians were. The Greek historian Herodotus stated: "Almost all of the names of Gods came into Greece from Egypt." Zeus was African and Venus was taken from the Egyptian goddess Hathor. Sappho (6th century B.C.E.) was the best lyric poet of Greece and described herself as being African.

Crete - An Aegean isle that was an important link between North Africa and Europe. Pottery discoveries show Libyan immigration to Crete in 4000 B.C.E., and large numbers of goddess-worshipping Libyan refugees from the western delta seem to have come to Crete when upper and lower Egypt were forcibly united during the 1st dynasty, approximately 3000 B.C.E. The first Minoan age began soon afterwards. Crete culture spread to Thrace and early Hellenic Greece. Ancient relationships between Crete and Egypt can be seen in the resemblance of the material culture between Egyptian and Minoan religion, especially in regards to the cults of the delta where double axes appear as a religious emblem. Also, Crete has retained traces of an African matrilineal system which can be seen in the pre-eminence of the goddess and by the prominence of women in Minoan Crete.

Italy - the ancient Romans were very much affected by African culture since they spent much of their time in some centuries either trying to conquer the Moors and the Egyptians, or keeping the Moors and Egyptians from conquering them. Twice in history and in separate millenniums, the Moors tried to conquer the Roman Empire. One of the most famous African conquerors who tried early on was Hannibal. The ancient Carthaginians fought three wars against Rome as mentioned earlier in this book, between 264-146 B.C.E., took control of the western half of Sicily and again came up to Italy as well as to Spain, Greece, etc. in the 6th century of this era (C.E.). Italy has been inhabited by Moors for hundreds of years since their occupation of the Roman city-states. The history of the culture, i.e. the wars fought, the songs and operas written about Moorish citizens, and the technology brought to Italy all indicate the contributions made by the Moors who took control of various parts of the Roman Empire. Their art and architectural influences can still be found in the countries that the Moors controlled such as in mosaics found in some of the ancient ruins of Sicily.

Britain: Ireland, Scotland, and England

The Moors left a long-standing influence on whatever culture they visited, and seemed to have not only influenced the culture of these islands, but also intermarried with various groups on those islands. Therefore, the racial heritage of those cultures is affected since many people, especially the Irish, mixed with the Moors during this period of Moorish domination. There are still people who are called Black-Irish living in Ireland due to their darker complexion and intermarriage with Africans who visited their isles some 1000 years ago. This is not the only influence those cultures have had on British culture. As the Moors visited various British islands in the North Atlantic, they brought musical instruments with them from North Africa and the Middle East. One instrument, the Bagpipe, is an instrument indigenous to North Africa as mentioned earlier in the book. That an instrument so totally characteristic of Africa, with its drone and reed structure, can find its way to such a vastly different culture, and then be viewed as a typical Scottish instrument is a credit to the spirit of exploration and innovation of the Moors and Arabs. Also the word Moor is still a common word used in the English language and is used frequently in the British culture.

Since Portugal is so close to Spain geographically and culturally, let us examine its history:

Portugal: Geographically speaking, Portugal, along with Spain and Greece is as close to Africa as it is to the continent that it belongs to. Portugal, as a part of the Iberian Peninsula, was subject to various attempts made by Moors and. Carthaginians, Arabs, and West African groups to conquer them. The Moors were successful in conquering various parts of what is now present-day Portugal and made agricultural, educational, scientific religious (Muslim) architectural, medical, and linguistic influences in the culture as well as mixing racially with the Portuguese people. Also, during one of the times that Portugal was conquered by African empires, Portuguese slaves were brought from Portugal to Africa.

Quotes on Spain

Portugal was described by Brunold Springer, a historian as "the 1st example of a Negrito (African) Republic in Europe." In the book <u>Racial Mixture as the Basic Principle of Life,</u> it is written: "Negroes had risen often to the caste of the nobility. Napoleon's army had small black Portuguese soldiers."

Africa begins at the Pyrenees

- 16th-century dictum by Cardinal Richelieu

"If Spain had kept her Moors, her agriculture and manufacturing would have prospered."

-from the book <u>Iberia</u>

"I will give you each a farm wherever you
choose to have it, either in Africa, Italy
or Spain."

Hannibal addressing his troops before the battle of Cannae.

X

Brasil

The history of Brazil is heavily intertwined with that of Africa. From the importation of slaves in the 17th century, to the practice of Condomble and from the resistance of slaves, some of whom revolted and returned to Africa, to the inextricably carved musical instruments and beautiful gowns designed by Brazilians of African descent; Brazil is a country tied to its motherland.

The history of African slaves from Angola in Brazil is an example of the exchange of culture that took place during the transatlantic slave trade era, where millions of Africans were forcibly transported to South America, with Brazil being one of the largest recipients of enslaved Black Africans.

Angola, located on the southwestern coast of Africa, was a major source of slaves for the Portuguese colonizers who settled in Brazil. The Portuguese began their exploration and colonization of Brazil in the early 16th century, and by the mid-1500s, they started importing large numbers of African slaves to meet the growing demand for labor on the sugar plantations and other agricultural enterprises.

Angolan slaves arrived in Brazil in vast numbers, making up a significant portion of the African population in the country. They were subjected to harsh conditions, exploitation, and abuse, enduring grueling labor on the plantations. The enslaved Angolans brought with them their own culture, traditions, and languages, and played a significant role in the development of Brazil's cultural heritage.

Over the centuries, these African slaves from Angola and their descendants helped shape Brazilian society, contributing to its music, dance, preferences, and religious practices. The blend of African, Native/indigenous Brazilian, and Portuguese influences gave rise to a unique Afro-Brazilian culture that remains a vibrant part of Brazil's identity to this day.

Manual Baimundo Querino, one of Brasil's most prominent African-Brazilian historians, was a prominent scholar in the field of Afro-Brazilian studies.

Manuel Querino (1851-1923) was an Afro-Brazilian intellectual, writer, and historian. He was born in Salvador, Bahia, the cultural capital of Brazil., He became a significant figure in the study of Afro-Brazilian history and culture during a time when the contributions of Black Brazilians were often overlooked.

Querino's most notable work is, "A Bahia de Outrora" ("The Bahia of Former Times"), published in 1916. This book delves into the history and culture of Bahia, shedding light on the significant role that people of African descent played in shaping the region's history including the development of Samba.

Manuel Querino's contributions have been valuable in promoting awareness of Afro-Brazilian heritage and history. He sought to challenge prevailing racial stereotypes and advocate for the recognition of the African roots in Brazil's cultural and social fabric.

His work remains influential in the study of Afro-Brazilian history and continues to inspire scholars and researchers to this day.

Brazil: With some of the most famous beaches on earth, Brazil's strength lies in its ability to take the languages, racial heritages, musical instruments, architectural, agricultural, and scientific technology brought to it by different cultural groups, and turn it into a cohesive should lead and exotic society. If one is to search for one specific region of the culture to determine where the most "Africanisms" are found and in what specific cultural characteristics, the place to look would have to be Bahia, and the characteristics to investigate are its music and religion. Religion Condomble is a religion practiced by a large segment of the population and is a thinly veiled African religion with African practices, and has Catholic names substituted for many of its deities, a practice begun during slavery. Music Many music forms were created in Bahia which would eventually travel to the rest of the country such as the Samba and carnival music. Brazilian music has influenced American Jazz and musicians all over the world. The mosaics on the boardwalks of Ipenema and Copacabana, in Rio de Janeiro, are indicative of the pride taken in the racial mixing of the. Society. The red, white, and gray mosaics on the boardwalks symbolize, as mentioned earlier in the book, the racial unity of the society. Brazil has architectural designs, such as is seen in the designs of various Catholic Churches, which are richly influenced by South American Indian culture.

Education Philosophers such as Paulo Freire, a product of Brazilian and Cape Verdian intermixing, have written essays and pedagogies on education and the oppressed, which are considered to be some of the world's most important philosophical writings on education as a means of conquering/freeing oneself from mental and physical oppression.

Brazilian: Literature

Antonio Gonzales Dias, 1823-1864 was a world-famous romantic poet from Brazil.

- Antonio Candido Goncalves Cresps, 1830-1882 was an outstanding Parnassian poet.

- Joaquim Maria Machado de Assis, 1839-1908 was the founder of the Brazilian Academy of Literature and was president for many years. He was an important representative of realism in Brazilian prose.

Religions found in Brasil

Condomble - This religion is an interesting mixture of West African tribal religions and Catholicism, and is practiced in Brazil.

Since slaves were not allowed to practice their own religions after being brought to Brazil, and were tortured if caught worshipping their African G-ds, and the slaves in Bahia and in other parts of Northeastern Brazil decided to find ways to practice their religion in spite of this cultural and religious persecution.

In some parts of Bahia, slaves escaped into the forest of the Amazon and established their own city-states where they were able to worship their own G-ds and trade goods and barter with the native South American tribes. In some instances, they even used their autonomy to return to their native homelands in Africa.

Other slaves who were not able to escape their plantations decided to mask the worship of their own G-ds by incorporating various Catholic beliefs into their own worship services.

When worshipping in the Portuguese slave-owners churches, the slaves would pretend that they were praying to the Catholic Saints.

Catholicism, with its emphasis on praying to holy men recognized by the church as intercessors for sins that have been committed, lends itself quite easily to substituting an African G-d for Catholic saints. When the Catholic slave-owners thought that the slaves had ceased practicing their "heathen" ways, in fact, the slaves were continuing to practice their own native African religions by incorporating the names of the Catholic saints into their own religions and worshipping their own G-ds who were now given Catholic names.

Vodun - This is a religion that began in Haiti and is now found in various parts of the Caribbean. It is probably one of the most well-known yet least understood of the African religions on earth and in this hemisphere. Vodun, like Candomblé, began as an attempt of the slaves to incorporate Catholic beliefs into their native African beliefs.

There is now further evidence that departs from the common assumption that Candomblé originated in the Yoruba (West African tribe) worship. The author of the book The Formation of Candomblé: Vodun History and Ritual in Brazil by Luis Nicolau Pares highlights the critical role of the Vodun religious practices in the formation and development of Condomble. Vodun traditions were brought by enslaved Africans of Dahomean origin from West Africa, to what is known as the "Jeje" nation in Brazil since the early eighteenth century. The book concludes with the author's account of present-day Jeje temples in Bahia, which serves as the first written record of the oral traditions and rituals of this particular nation of Candomblé.

Though there is an emphasis on the magical manipulation of one's environment; much of the portrayal of Vodun as is shown by the American entertainment industry (movies, etc.) is an exaggeration based on an attempt to make the American public feel that African religions are frightening and primitive. In reality followers of Vodun have regular worship services where they sing religious songs pray to their G-ds and have religious experiences.

XI

Other countries in Central and South America influenced by Africa

Venezuela: This country is comprised of people of mixed heritage who come from African slaves, Southern Europeans of Latin descent, and native South Americans. Parrandas, a festival performance of African origin, incorporates African idioms through dance music, songs, and performances using African instruments. That ceremony is performed regularly in that society.

Columbia: This country's population, as in most European and many South American countries, is a mixture of West African, Latin, and South American natives. The mixture makes up 68% of the country and is called Mestizos. Art forms that make this country one that is heavily influenced by Africa include Merengue - a dance and music form that was developed in the new world as an outgrowth of African music forms, and is a music form shared with other Caribbean isles.

Belize: It is a country that is technically a part of South America, as well as the Caribbean. Calypso music is the most popular music native of that country. The population is a mixture of European and African descendants and speaks Creole, a mixture of English and African words. Its music, religion, history, racial heritage, and language are heavily influenced by Africa.

XII

The Top Five Countries in the Caribbean Influenced by Africa

Trinidad & Tobago - located just a few miles off the coast of Venezuela, this island nation is world famous for its music, its African-influenced language, philosophy, festivals, and religious beliefs. Sharing a commonality of religious beliefs with other isles, Trinidad has its own venues of religious practices that are a mixture of Catholicism along with native West African religions. Trinidadians are descendants of West African slaves brought to that isle along with various European groups, East Indians, Arawaks, and other indigenous island groups. Shango is a local religion that uses drums to worship, and participants sing and chant during night services. Calypso music is native to Trinidad as is another form of music called Soca. Steel drum music also began in Trinidad.

Cuba: The music, the religions, the food, the genetic mixture, and the cultural ties are all indicative of the African influence on a nation in flux. The Cuban national dish consisting of white rice and black beans symbolizes the African mixed with the Spanish. The religion of Santeria, a mixture of West African beliefs and Catholicism, is heavily practiced by segments of the population as well as Vodun. The music is heavily influenced by Africa. Rhumba is a music form originating in Cuba that was developed by African slaves upon settling on that and surrounding islands. When the slaves were brought to Cuba, they celebrated their dances and their rhythms. As time went by, these African rhythms combined with the Spanish Flamenca music and formed the Cuban Rhumba. The Rhumba dancers of Cuba perceive this music to be a kind of medicine that, as one is taken over by the beat, begins to heal the body and soul. This musical tradition gets passed down from generation to generation, and is an undeniable blend of the African and Spanish cultures in Cuba. Also, Cuban dances such as the Mambo and the Cha Cha were imported into the U.S. early in this century. Those dances are derived from earlier Cuban dances that are mixtures of Spanish and African Rhythms and instruments. Needless to say, the country was colonized by the Spanish and inhabited by African slaves in the 1800's.

Puerto Rico: A country whose inhabitants are descendants of Latin Europeans, West Africans, and native islanders. It has a rich Latin tradition of music that uses African instruments and rhythm, coupled with Latin idioms and melodies sung in Spanish. Puerto Rico is a multicultural society whose music, racial heritage, and language are all indicative of its strong African influence.

Haiti: The first Black independent nation in the Western Hemisphere. This is one of the most heavily African-influenced countries in the western hemisphere. Haiti is not as heavily mixed racially as some Caribbean countries. Most people are descendants of slaves brought to the country from West Africa to work in the fields. There are a group of Haitians who are of mixed descent but for the most part, its citizens are of West African descent. The language spoken is French mixed with African dialects, but the music, history, artwork, philosophy, education, literature, and religion are all the result of transforming and transporting a culture from West Africa to a foreign land. Vodun as mentioned earlier in this book is a religion that began in Africa and is commonly practiced in Haiti. Many Haitian philosophers and writers have described their country as one in the midst of change, and in its universities, African history and law are studied alongside European centered academic disciplines.

Jamaica: herein is a sampling of some of the characteristics of the culture in Jamaica that are heavily African influenced:

1. Reggae music

2. Rasta Farianism

3. Jamaican Sculptured figures.

In its racial heritage, Jamaica is almost purely West African. It is a culture whose art forms so closely resemble West African ones that some people, (including myself and my former wife) saw some wooden figures in someone's home and remarked about how those West African figures reminded them of American works, whereupon they were told that those figures were Jamaican. Its people (as is the case in Haiti) are descendants of slaves, and have developed music forms, artwork, literature, religious beliefs, and language idioms that are African in nature if not African in inception.

Meringue was brought to the Americas by African slaves belonging to the Bara tribe from Madagascar who originally had a dance they called Meringue. Each Caribbean country gave this dance its own influence by including melodies of European origin. The words of Meringue are a description of the contemporary traditions of the society.

"IF A QUESTION WERE ASKED WHAT THE GREATEST ACHIEVEMENTS OF HUMANITY ARE, NO ANSWER COULD RIVAL.... THE DISCOVERY OF TIME, THE CONTROL AND USE OF FIRE, THE DEVELOPMENT OF TOOL TECHNOLOGY, LANGUAGE AND AGRICULTURE. NOTHING IN THE 20TH CENTURY HAS TOUCHED HUMANITY SO TOTALLY AS THOSE THINGS WHICH WERE FIRST ACCOMPLISHED BY AFRICANS."

– PORTLAND OREGON BASELINE ESSAYS ON HUMANITY.

"IF EUROPE IS THE OLD WORLD, THEN AFRICA IS THE MOTHER OF THE HUMAN SPECIES, THE ORIGINATOR OF CIVILIZATION, AND THE CULTIVATOR OF THE CONCEPT OF ESTHETICISM. IN ESSENCE, AFRICA CAN BE SEEN AS THE TOTALITY OF HOW WE PERCEIVE OURSELVES AS BELONGING TO MOTHER EARTH."

– GISM

"SALT COMES FROM THE NORTH, GOLD FROM THE SOUTH AND SILVER FROM THE COUNTRY OF THE WHITE MAN, BUT THE WORD OF G-D AND THE TREASURES OF WISDOM CAN ONLY BE FOUND AT TIMBUCTU."

– SUDANESE PROVERB

XIII

Moses & Israel

At the opposite end of the Mediterranean is another crossroads. If Spain is where Europe meets Africa, Israel is where Asia meets Africa, and the results are a culture composed of tribes who migrated back and forth, and from Africa to Palestine and back in quest of a secure homeland for their people. Any discussion of the influence of Africa on Moses needs to discuss the land of Israel, and the forefathers and mothers of that culture can be traced back to Abraham. History having secured land for his people, Abraham lived in Palestine. His descendants moved to Africa and lived there for several centuries seeking refuge from a drought in the land of Canaan. Upon being oppressed by an indigenous group of Africans who had, at first, warmly greeted the 12 tribes, they were led back to Palestine by Moses who was educated in the Egyptian Pharoah's court, and who married a Nubian and lived in the Sinai Peninsula before meeting his destiny. He was considered the greatest of all Jewish leaders who "codified Jewish law." Probably no other culture as ancient as Israel has had such a long-term relationship with Africa. On the other hand, since Africa contains the oldest of civilizations, it would be logical that many of ancient Israel's earliest, most continuous, and most important interactions would take place with African peoples. There is ample evidence of ancient cultural interactions between Israel, Egypt, and various African societies. The ancient land of Canaan, which includes modern-day Israel, was geographically situated at the crossroads of Africa, Asia, and Europe. As a result, it became a meeting point for diverse cultures and civilizations. Scholarly journals, such as the Journal of Ancient Egyptian Interconnections have documented the anthropological evidence of the interactions and connections between Israel, Egypt and Africa. It began with the 12 tribes moving to Israel, the diplomatic (& personal) relationship between Solomon and The Queen of Sheba (who instituted the practice of Judaism in a large section of East Africa), and continued with the Moorish rule over Southern Europe and Spanish Jewry. Also, the Moors explored and conquered the Mediterranean area of Eurasia. A continuous relationship with Africa has been maintained by Israelis as Africans passed through Israel and conquered and explored Asia.

Israel: The early history of the ancient Hebrew tribes is clearly tied to Africa. One clear indication of this can be found in the relationships and intermarriages that took place between them and the Canaanites and the Ethiopians. Jewish philosophy was influenced by Egypt. While in captivity, Hebrews such as Maimonides studied in Africa, and Moors dominated Jewish culture in Spain. In fact, Maimonides, who was born in Córdoba, Spain in 1135 spent much of his life in various places in the Islamic world, including Morocco and Egypt. Though Western scholars continue to insist that this region of Africa is considered part of the Middle East and North Africa, a central premise of this book is the original tribes of Morrocco and Egypt in particular are a part of, and inextricably connected to the peoples of sub-Saharan Africa, and whose genetic ancestors of the Egyptian Pharaohs can be traced to Africa. The genetic and anthropological evidence supports the idea that a number of Egyptian Pharaohs, including Ramses III, had their royal bloodline traced back to the Upper Nile region of Egypt and Nubia (present-day southern Egypt and northern Sudan).

Evidence from mitochondrial DNA analysis of ancient Egyptian mummies has shown affinities with populations from the Near East, sub-Saharan Africa, and the local Nile Valley region. Additionally, Y-chromosome DNA analysis has provided evidence of genetic connections between ancient Egyptians and populations from northeastern Africa and the Middle East.

Studies have identified genetic affinities between ancient Egyptian mummies and present-day populations in the region, including those from the Upper Nile region of Egypt and Nubia. The Kingdom of Kush, which was located in Nubia, south of Egypt, interacted closely with ancient Egypt over several millennia, leading to significant cultural and genetic exchanges between the two civilizations.

The 20th Dynasty of Egypt, during which Ramses III ruled, was one of the most prominent periods of interaction between Egypt and Nubia. Ramses III himself had a significant number of Nubian individuals in his court and military, reflecting the close ties between the two regions.

Overall, genetic and anthropological evidence supports the notion that some Egyptian Pharaohs, including Ramses III, had their royal bloodline traced back to the Upper Nile region of Egypt and Nubia, reflecting the complex and interconnected history of ancient Egypt and the surrounding regions.

Africans explored and conquered Israel, and Jewish writers referred to Africa in their writings. After having settled in Africa during the time of Moses, the Israeli tribes adopted an African Familial Classification System (the 12 tribes of Israel) They also adopted an African religious theology called monotheism (the belief in one G-d), a concept practiced and developed by the Egyptians during that same time in history. For instance, during the time of Moses and the Exodus narrative, the Israelites were exposed to Egyptian religious concepts and practices during their time in Egypt, which influenced elements of their own religious beliefs including the concept of the One True God. **The Moses Mystery: The African Origins of the Jewish People** by Gary Greenberg, and **Moses: A Life** by Jonathan Kirsch both discuss the influence of Egyptian culture and religion on his beliefs.

Saudi Arabia: The Arabian Peninsula (especially, South Arabia) was occupied by Ethiopian Army troops during the reign of the Ethiopian empire.

Religion

Judaism - This religion was codified by an African, Moses, whose job it was to ensure that the Torah or Law of Moses as orally revealed to him by the creator, was passed to each future generation of the Jewish people.

Judaism has been practiced by the Jewish people for almost 6,000 years. During that period of time in history, many Jews who were merchants, diplomats, politicians, soldiers of fortune, or travelers moved to and lived in Africa due to the close geographic proximity of North and East Africa to the ancient Israeli empire.

From a geographic standpoint, the Sinai Peninsula including the land of Palestine can really be considered a part of Africa. While in

Africa, the Jews built Temples and Synagogues to study in (see the section on Africa and the Bible and Elephantine).

Also, several East African empires practiced Judaism beginning during the rule of King Solomon, who had strong diplomatic, political, and economic ties to the ancient Ethiopian empire (see section on the Queen of Sheba).

Islam - Disciples of Mohammed began coming into North Africa 700 years ago, and vehemently persuaded anyone they encountered to worship Allah or die. Their cultural influence on northern and western Africa was so strong that many North African nations not only took on the tenets of Islam; they also adopted the written language (Arabic), and the customs of those who brought the religion to them. Islam is one of the primary religions practiced in West Africa, and is the most commonly practiced religion in all of North Africa. African countries heavily populated by Arab Muslims include: Morocco, Sudan, Libya, Algeria, and Tunisia.

XIV

The List of religious Concepts Originating in Africa

Monotheism- Moses is thought to be the first person to espouse the concept of the belief in one G-d and formulate a religion based on that concept.

Yet, during that same time in history, and in the same country (Kemite), another person also raised in the Pharaoh's court was in the process of adhering to or believing in the same concept. To get an accurate picture of what was happening in that part of the world in the year 5000 B.C.E. let's briefly examine the cultural/religious developments taking place in that era.

Several hundred years before Moses was born the Kemites had begun to discuss the possibility of the existence of one supreme G-d. Off and on during that time period, various kings and Pharaohs would proclaim this belief in one deity as being more powerful than all others. Therefore, by the time Moses was born, the concept of one supreme deity had already been introduced and accepted as a theological possibility in that culture.

The next question becomes how Moses heard of this concept. The answer to this question is simple: The <u>Bible</u> tells us that Moses was raised in the Pharaoh's court and given an African education. He was probably quite familiar with African monotheism, and was already comfortable with the idea of believing in the concept of one G-d when the Creator of all things (Blessed be the name of Adonai) spoke into his ear the Law or Torah.

The other person espousing the idea of monotheism was Amenhotep IV, who later named himself Akhenaton, Pharaoh of Kemite, who married Queen Nefertiti, established the holy city of Amarna, and was succeeded by King Tut. He ascended to the throne in the year 1387 B.C.E. and ruled Kemite from the year 1387 to 1366 B.C.E.

While ruling the kingdom of Egypt, Amenhotep IV decided that there is but one G-d, Aton the sun, who gives life, and is superior to all other G-ds. His belief in this deity was so strong that he built a city of worship called Amarna near the capital of Kemite where people could come and worship this one G-d.

The establishment of the city of Amarna was such an important historical event that scholars now call that period in history following his reign the Amarna period.

The Amarna age is named after the ruins of the capital that Akhenaton built, in dedication to Aton who he believed to be the one true G-d. During that time in history, government officials in Amarna wrote letters to minor politicians in various states controlled by the

Kemites such as ancient Israel, the land of the Hittites, etc. The Amarna Age is known for the following important events:

I.   The exodus of the 12 tribes of Israel from Egypt.

II.   The conquest and occupation of the land of Canaan by the 12 tribes of Israel.

III.   The life of Moses.

IV.   The compiling of the first five books of the <u>Bible</u>.

V.   The rule of King Tut.

VI.   The emergence of the Babylonian empire.

The next reasonable question becomes: did Moses and Amenhotep meet each other or know of each other's ideas? From what we know about their two lives, Moses and Amenhotep may have been briefly alive during the same time in history. Did they have a chance to discuss their views with each other? We may never know the answer to that question.

QUOTE FROM THE BOOK OF <u>ZEPHANIAH</u>, THE <u>BIBLE</u>

"From beyond the rivers of Ethiopia shall they bring my suppliants. Even the daughters of my dispersed as mine offering."

XV

Africa and the Bible

Descendants of Abraham, Isaac, and Jacob have had a long and continuous relationship with the continent of Africa. I will begin this section by simply listing each person connected to, or involved in some way, with Africa either through genetic heritage, marriage, or by having lived part or all of their lives on the continent. I will use the Bible as the main, and sometimes only, documenting source.

XVI

THE LIST OF FAMOUS BIBLICAL CHARACTERS ASSOCIATED WITH AFRICA

ABRAHAM: He lived in Canaan, a region that at that time in history was inhabited by people of Black African descent. He bore a child by his Egyptian concubine (Hagar) named Ishmael, a famous Biblical character. Ishmael would later have Esau, who would become the father of the Arab tribes. This indicates a direct linkage between the Arab race and Africa.

MOSES: He lived in the royal palace in Kemite as the adopted son of Queen Hatshepsut, the daughter of Thutmose I. Moses was raised by Black Africans and educated by the royal family in Egypt (Kemite), which was at that time inhabited by Africans of Nubian descent. Moses lived his entire life in Africa, except at the very end when he led his people from the Sinai desert to the land of Canaan (a land that he was not allowed to step foot on incidentally). Moses married a Midianite woman of Nubian descent named Zipporah when he fled Egypt. They had two sons named Gershom and Eliezer who most likely married Midianite women and lived with other Africans. Moses left Kemite for 40 years to escape prosecution for a criminal act he had committed.

DAVID: A major battle that made him famous was against Goliath and the Philistines, who were descendants of Cush, and according to the Bible (Genesis) were Black.

GOLIATH: He fought a major battle against David, King of the Israeli empire. As mentioned above, Goliath was a Philistine and a descendant of the Kushites.

SOLOMON: This son of King David became King of Israel upon his father's death. As word spread of his wisdom, many heads of state in surrounding regions decided to visit him including an African Queen of the ancient land of Cush named Sheba or Makeba. As a result of her royal visit to Israel, King Solomon and the Queen of Sheba fell in love and thus, began one of the world's first royal (and most famous) love affairs. Israel and the land of Sheba had an extensive and long interaction throughout history, and active diplomatic relations took place between the two governments due to their love affair - a chapter is forthcoming.

YESHUA Ha Messiah: (Jesus the Christ) lived in Africa as a child when his parents brought him to Egypt to escape religious persecution. During his early childhood, and in later years, he was heavily influenced by the Gnostic teachings of the African mystics. Also, since he was a descendant of the royal line of King David and King Solomon, he is a distant but direct cousin to the Solominic line of Kings who ruled Ethiopia for thousands of years.

The Apostle THOMAS: This disciple of Christ went south to Kemite (Egypt) and East Africa after having preached the good news of Christ's life and resurrection. His visit to Egypt and Ethiopia led to the establishment of the first Church outside of Israel, the Coptic Church of Egypt, and the Ethiopian or Abyssinian Church of Ethiopia.

PHAROAH, King of Egypt during Moses' time in Israel: Since Kemite was ruled by Africans of Nubian descent during the time of Moses, the king of Egypt who refused to let the 12 tribes leave Egypt must also have been of Nubian descent.

HAM: He is one of the sons of Noah and the ancestor to the tribes that inhabit Northeast Africa, according to the Random House Dictionary.

CANAAN: He is the father of the Canaanites and Phoenicians - the original inhabitants of Palestine. The Canaanites were conquered by the Israelites and absorbed and enslaved by them, according to the Bible Almanac which means that the 12 tribes of Israel conquered, lived with, and intermarried with a native African people.

CUSH: He is the father of the Ethiopian tribes who inhabited the lands to the south of Egypt in eastern Africa.

ZEPHANIAH: A Jewish prophet who accurately prophesized that there would be Jewish colonies beyond the rivers of Nubia.

INTERESTING FACTS ABOUT AFRICA AND ANCIENT ISRAEL NOT IN THE BIBLE

The Philistines, who were Black Africans as mentioned earlier in the book, hired Israelites from the tribe of Dan to be seafarers for their empire. The Jews working for this empire conducted trade as far south as the Horn of Africa.

Architecture

The first temple outside of Israel (Jerusalem) was established on an island off the coast of Africa called Elephantine on the Nile River. It was a Jewish colony, and was the ancient border between Egypt and Nubia in the year 500 B.C.E. near the modern city of Aswan.

Then the 12 Hebrew clans who were descendants of Abraham began to call themselves the 12 tribes, and this tribal classification began after living in Egypt for several hundred years. What other cultural characteristics had they picked up while living in Africa - the motherland?

XVIII

THE LIST OF FAMOUS BIBLICAL LANDS INHABITED BY BLACK AFRICANS (Palestine)

Not only was one of Abraham's concubines African making Isaac's half-brother of African descent; when the Jewish people conquered the land of Canaan after they left Kemite, the <u>Bible</u> as well as the <u>Random House Dictionary</u> documents that the Hebrew tribes absorbed the Canaanites, as mentioned earlier in this book. The book called **The Canaanites: The People of the Land of Canaan According to the Old Testament and Biblical Belles-Lettres by B.T.A. Evetts.** Since the Canaanites were closely associated with native Africans, it is safe to state that from that period on the Jewish people began to be, from a racial standpoint, Asian/African people.

"WHEN ASIA OVERWHELMED EGYPT, EGYPT SOUGHT REFUGE IN ETHIOPIA (NUBIA) AS A CHILD RETURNS TO ITS MOTHER, AND ETHIOPIA THEN FOR CENTURIES DOMINATED EGYPT AND SUCCESSFULLY INVADED ASIA."

W.E.B. DUBOIS, THE WORLD AND AFRICA: AN INQUIRY INTO THE PART WHICH AFRICA HAS PLAYED IN WORLD HISTORY, NEW YORK: INTERNATIONAL PUBLISHERS, 1961, P.117.

"I LEARNED THAT ALONG WITH THE TOWERING ACHIEVEMENTS OF THE CULTURES OF ANCIENT GREECE AND CHINA THERE STOOD THE CULTURE OF AFRICA, UNSEEN AND DENIED BY THE IMPERIALIST LOOTERS OF AFRICA'S MATERIAL WEALTH."

– PAUL ROBESON

"SIR," BANNEKER WROTE, "... IF YOUR LOVE FOR YOURSELVES, AND FOR THOSE INESTIMABLE LAWS WHICH PRESERVE TO YOU THE RIGHTS OF HUMAN NATURE, WAS FOUNDED ON SINCERITY, YOU COULD NOT BUT BE SOLICITOUS THAT EVERY INDIVIDUAL OF WHATEVER RANK OR DISTINCTION, MIGHT WITH YOU EQUALLY ENJOY THE BLESSINGS THEREOF, NEITHER COULD YOU REST SATISFIED... [UNTIL] THEIR PROMOTIONS FROM ANY STATE OF DEGRADATION TO WHICH THE UNJUSTIFIABLE CRUELTY AND BARBARISM OF MEN MAY HAVE REDUCED THEM. ... I AM OF THE AFRICAN RACE AND IN THAT COLOR WHICH IS NATURAL TO THEM OF THE DEEPEST DYE, AND IT IS UNDER A SENSE OF THE MOST PROFOUND GRATITUDE TO THE SUPREME RULER OF THE UNIVERSE, THAT I AM NOT UNDER THAT STATE OF TYRANNICAL THRALLDOM, AND INHUMAN CAPTIVITY, TO WHICH TOO MANY OF MY BRETHREN ARE DOOMED."

– BENJAMIN BANNEKER

"HERE WAS SAID AND IS WIDE MINGLING OF THE BLOOD OF ALL RACES IN AFRICA, BUT THOUGH IS CONSISTENT WITH THE GENERAL THESIS THAT AFRICA IS PREDOMINANTLY THE LAND OF NEGROES AND NEGROID PEOPLES, JUST AS EUROPE IS A LAND OF CAUCASOIDS AND ASIA OF MONGOLOIDS. WE MAY GIVE UP ENTIRELY, IF WE WITH, THE WHOLE ATTEMPT TO DELIMIT RACES, BUT WE CANNOT IF WE ARE SANE, DIVIDE THE WORLD INTO WHITES, YELLOWS AND BLACKS, AND THEN CALL BLACKS WHITES."

– W.E.B. DUBOIS

IN SPITE OF THE FACT THAT THE AFRICAN SLAVE'S CULTURE, LANGUAGE, AND PAST HISTORY WERE SYSTEMICALLY DESTROYED/ELIMINATED IN THE AMERICAS; DESPITE THE FACT THAT THE RESULTING CULTURAL GENOCIDE HAD A PROFOUND NEGATIVE IMPACT ON THE COLLECTIVE PSYCHE OF BLACK AMERICANS DURING AND AFTER RECONSTRUCTION AND WAS EXPRESSED THROUGH THE MUSIC, ART AND WRITINGS OF THE CULTURAL RENAISSANCE; DESPITE FACING ALL THESE OBSTACLES, BLACK AMERICANS MANAGED TO CHANGE THE SOCIAL INFRASTRUCTURE OF THE MOST POWERFUL NATION THAT HAS EVER EXISTED. THE NEXT SECTION OF THIS BOOK WILL EXPLAIN HOW AND WHY THAT HAPPENED.

E. GERONIMO ROBINSON

XIX

Coltrane and
The United States of America

Probably in no other country in the western hemisphere can such a profound African influence be felt. What makes this influence so ironic is that of all the countries in the western hemisphere that had slavery, America was the most rigid in its requirement that the slaves from Africa did not practice their native customs and religions, speak their native languages, retain historical information about their cultures, or bring their musical instruments from Africa to America.

Yet, in spite of these incredible cultural obstacles, settlers and slaves of West African descent managed to bring and transpose their African culture to America, and ultimately transformed America into a highly unique artistic and technologically advanced society. This society became composed of an intermingling of Native American,

Western, and Southern (African) civilizations. I will now list a sampling of the vast influence that Africans have had on America.

<u>Religion</u> the African Methodist Episcopal Church

The Christian Methodist Episcopal Church

The Pentecostal Movement (precursor to the Born Again Movement)

The Black Baptist Church

The Black Jewish groups

The Black Muslim Movement

All these groups have strongly influenced this society. The Black Muslim Movement has caused America to recognize that Blacks can have religious movements separate from the Judeo-Christian ethic recognized in this country as the norm from which American Churches arose.

Some of these religious leaders were radicals, separate from the American mainstream. Many progressive African-American authors have written various essays attacking racism and classism in this country. They have advocated the overthrow of the American class system as well as promoting the achievement of personal and economic freedom from oppression and racism.

The Black Christian Movement, which became intertwined with the Civil Rights Movement during the 1950s and onward, preached recognition of Jim Crow laws as being symptomatic of a disease-filled society. In order to change the sick brethren who are racist, Black activists preached that love must be unleashed upon hate, righteousness upon oppression, justice against injustice.

The African Methodist Episcopal Church was founded in 1816 by Richard Allen, a former slave and a member of a white Methodist church. He refused to continue worshipping in a church where the congregation was segregated based on their race (with the Black worshipers sitting in the back), while a doctrine of unconditional love for all people was being preached during each sermon. He left the church and created the African Methodist Episcopal (A.M.E.) Church with a group of other former slaves.

The A.M.E. Zion Church and the C.M.E. (Christian Methodist Episcopal) Church are descendants of the A.M.E. Church. Famous activists and leaders of conscious who were members of the A.M.E. Church include Frederick Douglas, Harriet Tubman, and Sojourner Truth.

The Black Pentecostal movement in the United States is a reflection of the strong emphasis on rhythm and the use of percussive instruments, both during musical selections and while worshipers are chanting and praying.

The African influence can also be seen in the highly expressive manner in which Black Pentecostals, as well as Black Baptists conduct their worship services. In their worship service, communication with G-d is viewed as a means of expressing one's feelings about fear and death and songs, and chants convey the feelings and world view of the worshippers by testifying about the nearness of G-D.

Education

Black Americans founded many universities and colleges, such as Bennett College that would produce Black intellectuals that would affect every area of American life. Black Universities produced Dr. King, former Justice Thurgood Marshall, Andy Young, and Duke Ellington within the first 40 years of this century.

Illiteracy was down to 3 and 4% in Black communities in major American cities such as St. Louis for example, in the early 1920s (according to Harvard historian David Tyack, author of **One Best System**). This was largely due to the efforts of Black American educators, and the segregated African-American school system at that time in ourstory/herstory.

This interest in education and the creation of schools that would produce such an incredible cadre of famous civil rights leaders, music composers, and scientists speaks well of the continuation of the emphasis on the university in the Black community, as a means of educating their people, a concept originally African in nature.

Music

Black Americans have had a profound influence on music, not only through Rock and Roll etc., but also through performers and composers such as Elvis Presley, whose musical style and dance moves are undeniably taken from and imitate Black American performers such as Bo Diddley. Elvis Presley, often referred to as the "King of Rock and Roll," was clearly influenced by Bo Diddley, along with other well-known Black American musicians of his time including Little Richard and Fats Domino. Bo Diddley, a legendary rhythm and blues musician, was known for his distinctive style, creativity, and incorporating African rhythms and beats into his own amazing showmanship, and unique guitar-playing style.

The following is a list of the music forms in America that were developed by Black Americans as a consequence of being in America, and which convey or communicate the feelings Black Americans had about being in the Diaspora (outside Africa). This includes the following characteristics;

Syncopation of rhythm,

call and response techniques,

An emphasis on imitation of musical sounds emanating from musical instruments etc.

Characteristics of African American Music

- Vocal imitation of instruments (Jazz)

- Instrumental imitation of voice (Jazz)

- Use of strong rhythmic patterns in the melody

- Description of religious concepts in the music's lyrics

- Use of string instruments as part of the rhythmic continuity of a song, and in use in a love song.

This list does not include music forms such as Country and Western music which was influenced by Africans. The banjo, for example, was heavily used by country western singers, and was brought to America by African slaves.

Discussing the origin of Jazz as an American Music form, Dizzy Gillespie and Charlie Parker are considered to be 2 of the more prominent and important Jazz musicians of the 20th century. The sound they created was called Be Bop. These 2 musical giants are viewed by many scholars who study the origin of this genre of music to have played a profound role in the creation of the African-American Classical music aesthetic that is called Jazz. Here is an interview of those 2 Jazz musician giants who discuss how they created synergy together, and had a significant role to play in the creation of the music form that is revered around the world, and is considered to be America's only true Classical music form.

Dizzy Gillespie: "Cause I'D been in New York all the time and he brought Charlie Parker in this hotel room in the Booker Washington Hotel."

Charlie Parker: "There was nothing to do but play you know and we had a lot of fun trying to play you know."

Dizzy Gillespie: "Right after that Charlie Parker was mine."

Charlie Parker: That was the first time I ever had the pleasure to meet Dizzy Gillespie."

Dizzy Gillespie: "I remember Miles...."

Charlie Parker: "Miles was in my original band."

Dizzy Gillespie: "....and Charlie Parker created the sound and the moment I heard him I said (finger snap) that's how music should sound."

From Quincy Jones' 1990 Grammy award winning album `Back on the Block'.

XX

The List of Western Music Forms Derived from Africa

The Following is a List of American/Western Music Forms Whose Musical Characteristics are Derived from Africa:

- Jazz - Bop, Bebop, Modern Jazz etc.
- Blues
- Ragtime
- Dixieland
- Soul
- Funk
- Gospel
- Rhythm & Blues
- Rock & Roll

- Cajun music
- Pop
- Disco
- Spiritual

Caribbean

- Reggae
- Calypso
- Soca
- Salsa

South American

- Samba
- Carnival music
- Meringue
- Rhumba

XXI

The Brief List of European Instruments brought to the West by Africans

- Harp
- Banjo
- Bagpipe
- Drum
- Violin

XXII

The List of Dance Forms Created by Persons of African Descent

- Charleston

- Cakewalk

- Lindy hop

- Jitterbug

- Breakdancing

- Capoeira

- Skimma

- Turkey trot

- Samba

- Merenque

- Cuban Rhumba

- Mambo

- Soca

XXIII

The List of Cities
where Jazz Originated

- New Orleans

- Chicago

- St. Louis

- Kansas City, Kansas

- New York City

- Richmond, Va.

- Memphis

- Philadelphia

XXIV

The List of Six World Class Artists of African Descent

Marian Anderson - A legendary contralto opera singer. Diva Marian Anderson paved the way for all future American opera stars of African descent through her incredible interpretations of some of the world's great operatic works by composers such as Verdi and Puccini, and her willingness to prevail during a time in history when the U.S.A. restricted her ability to perform in American concert halls due to segregation laws in the early 1900s.

A particularly famous incident of note occurred when the Daughters of the American Revolution refused to allow her to perform at Constitution Hall in Washington D.C., even after many protests from local African American civil rights groups etc.

Ms. Anderson finally performed on the steps of the Lincoln Memorial, in what was to become one of her most famous and historically important concerts in 1939.

Leontyne Price - One of the world's great soprano opera singers. Educated at Julliard, Ms. Price has premiered the works of Stravinsky, Barber, and Montaine, has won 19 Grammys, and is the winner of the Presidential Medal of Freedom.

Leontyne Price is one of the great divas of this or any century.

Paul Robeson - World renowned Shakespearean actor, civil rights activist, opera singer and athlete. Paul Robeson was a renaissance man who spoke dozens of languages, practically invented the concept of the Off-Broadway Play in New York city, and introduced the Negro Spiritual music form to International audiences in Europe, Asia and, South America.

William Grant Still - One of the great classical composers of the early 1900s. Mr. Still composed scores for ballets, orchestras, and musicals in the early part of this century, which made him a musical trailblazer in the earlier part of the century since African Americans were seldom given the opportunity to compose musical scores for major theatrical productions at that time.

Katherine Dunham - A choreographer and dedicated anthropologist. Ms. Dunham is one of the great dance innovators of this century, and is responsible for bringing Caribbean rhythms to the American stage, as well as creating the first professional Black dance company in America. She is largely responsible for the worldwide recognition of the Black dance aesthetic.

John Coltrane - Seldom does an artist exist in any given century with the kinds of skills and talents of Mr. Coltrane, yet he is an astonishing example of the musical geniuses given birth by the African American female descendants of North American slaves. Mr. Coltrane is one the great instrumentalists and performers of Bebop music, who has or will ever live. His re-interpretation of such American musical favorites as `My Favorite Things' is considered by musical scholars to be indicative of the high level of complexity of African American Atonal music. John Coltrane belongs to a small group of musical innovators who have influenced music worldwide. On the next page we will discuss:

XXV

John Coltrane and his influence on American music and culture

Coltrane was a legendary American jazz saxophonist and composer whose contributions had a profound impact on the development of jazz as a major American music form. Here are some of the key ways in which Coltrane influenced jazz:

1. **Innovative Playing Style**: Coltrane was a virtuoso saxophonist known for his innovative and technically advanced playing style. He extended the range and capabilities of the saxophone, particularly the tenor and soprano saxophones, through his masterful use of overtones, multiphonics, and rapid note patterns. His ability to navigate complex chord progressions and employ extended harmonies set him apart from his contemporaries.

2. **Modal Jazz**: Coltrane was a pioneer of modal jazz, a style that focused on using musical modes (scales) rather than traditional chord progressions. This approach provided greater freedom for improvisation and allowed musicians to explore new harmonic possibilities. His landmark album "Giant Steps" (1960) is considered a classic example of his modal jazz compositions.

3. **A Love Supreme**: One of Coltrane's most influential works is his album "A Love Supreme" (1965). This spiritual and deeply personal work showcased his commitment to using music as a means of spiritual expression. The album's four-part suite, with its powerful improvisations and emotive melodies, had a lasting impact on jazz, and continues to be revered as a masterpiece. That particular album is considered one of the most creative and groundbreaking albums of the 20th century.

4. **Free Jazz**: Coltrane's later period saw him experimenting with "free jazz," a style characterized by extended improvisation without predetermined chord changes or structures. This experimental phase, exemplified in albums like "Ascension" (1966) and "Interstellar Space" (1967), challenged the boundaries of traditional jazz and paved the way for future avant-garde jazz movements.

5. **Collaborations**: Coltrane worked with other influential jazz musicians, including Thelonious Monk, Miles Davis, and McCoy Tyner. These collaborations allowed for the cross-pollination of ideas and styles, further pushing the boundaries of jazz and leading to the evolution of new sounds. John Coltrane actually was a member of Miles Davis' earlier Jazz Quartets, and one can thank Miles Davis for giving Coltrane a platform to have the kind of creative freedom he needed to experiment with his own style as he became a Jazz giant.

6. **Influence on Future Generations**: Coltrane's innovative playing style, modal approach, and explorations into free jazz significantly influenced subsequent generations of jazz musicians. His impact can be heard in the works of artists like Pharoah Sanders, Alice Coltrane (his wife), and many other avant-garde and contemporary jazz musicians.

7. **Legacy**: Coltrane's legacy extends far beyond his lifetime. He remains one of the most revered figures in jazz history, and his recordings continue to inspire and captivate audiences worldwide. His dedication to pushing the boundaries of jazz, and his pursuit of spiritual expression through music solidified his place as one of the most influential figures in the development of jazz as a major American music form.

In summary, John Coltrane's contributions to jazz as a major American music form are immeasurable and immense. His innovative playing style, modal and free jazz explorations, and collaborations with some of the most prolific and talented Jazz composers and musicians of the 20th century had a lasting impact on future generations of jazz musicians. His legacy continues to solidify his position as one of the genre's most influential and talented musicians and composers.

XXVI

The List of Great American Jazz Composers and Performers of African Descent

The list of Jazz innovators include Dizzy Gillespie, Thelonius Monk, Edward Kennedy Ellington, Charlie Parker, Miles Davis, Max Roach, Sonny Rollins, Roy Eldridge, and Charlie Mingus.

The List of Great American Jazz Composers & Performers of African Descent are as follows:

- Fletcher Henderson
- Count Basie
- Lester Young
- Charlie Parker
- Louis Armstrong

- Duke Ellington
- Roy Eldridge
- Benny Goodman
- Thelonius Monk
- Max Roach
- Sonny Rollins
- Sarah Vaughan
- Betty Carter
- Mary Lou Williams
- Charlie Mingus
- Billy Eckstine
- Dizzie Gillespie
- Miles Davis
- Ella Fitzgerald
- George Benson
- Bo Diddley
- Eubie Blake
- Ella Fitzgerald
- Bessie Smith
- Quincy Jones
- Jelly Roll Morton

In the next several sections of the book, this author discusses how Black Americans have dominated the fields of science, civil rights/ philosophy/law, literature, and sports throughout the 19th and 20th centuries. Black American scientists are usually marginalized, but have made major contributions to the field of science. Black American civil rights leaders have contributed to, and are responsible for, America becoming closer to fulfilling its promise of being a democracy. One of my main philosophical goals in my career has been the notion that Black American has made this country no longer dependent on racism as a primary basis for social construct, and it should be reiterated that Black Americans are responsible for *changing and influencing the social, political and cultural infrastructure of American society.* Black American lawyers made education accessible for all Americans, and forced this country to tear down its legal mandates of separate but equal. Black American athletes continue to excel and dominate US Football, basketball, tennis, and other sports including the Olympics on an international level, and Black American community has produced several of the greatest Athletes in the history of the 20th and 21st centuries, including Muhammad Ali, Joe Louis, Michael Jordan, Tiger Woods, The Williams sisters in tennis, Lebron James, Simone Biles and Coco Gauff. There are monuments to American civil rights in Europe at Westminster Abbey in London, and streets in Caribbean countries named after MLK.

The influence of Black Americans in Science and Medicine is listed below.

The United States of America is a more technologically advanced society due to the contributions of Black American scientists, etc. In every facet of the development of American technology, black inventors, scientists, etc. have been involved, and have made the US an international powerhouse of innovation, scientific discovery, and medical breakthroughs. Black doctors were the first to do open-heart surgery and separate plasma from blood (Charles Drew).

Agriculture scientists such as George Washington Carver experimented with new forms of beans, and invented synthetic soybeans; and architects such as Benjamin Banneker designed the nation's capital using an incomplete layout left by French engineer Pierre Charles L'Enfant, chief architect of the District of Columbia who resigned during the earlier stages of the design of the city. Mr. Banneker also wrote almanacs and designed an extremely accurate time clock.

African Americans were inventors, scholars, doctors, lawyers, poets, and classical composers. Men such as Garrett Morgan saved thousands of men's lives during WWI by inventing the gas mask. He also created urban and rural local community travel rules, and structures for American communities by inventing the stop light. Black American Female engineers and scientists who worked for NASA played major roles in sending the first humans to the Moon, as is chronicled and shown in the movie aptly named, "Hidden Figures" since most of the contributions Black American scientists and inventors have made in US History have been hidden, and/or ignored, or simply erased from US history books.

Civil Rights

Scholars such as Franklin, Dubois, and Amira Baraka chronicled American life, and Black American and African history, so that the entire world would be able to observe the plight and struggle of Black Americans in their quest for dignity.

Sociologists such as W.E.B. Dubois analyzed American history and surmised that the only way Black Americans can make important contributions, and become successful partners in the American mainstream, is through educating themselves, becoming professionals in a chosen field, and becoming intellectuals.

Other Black leaders such as Booker T. Washington felt that Blacks needed to learn a vocation, a skill that would lead to meaningful employment and self-empowerment. He was not concerned about intellectual enlightenment, or social integration into the American mainstream. Though they were at odds with each other while alive, Dubois and Washington both made eloquent and meaningful arguments for their cases.

Other leaders who were to become world famous, such as Marcus Garvey preached a new type of Black Nationalism that would affect Black America, as well as Caribbean Blacks.

Garvey spoke of Blacks returning to Africa, and leaving behind the racism and non-acceptance of the white community of Blacks in the economic, political, and social infrastructure of the society.

Black Americans, or specifically Americans of Black African descent, have made a significant impact on the history and social class structure of this country.

Never before in history has one group of oppressed people been so vocal, and so willing to risk their lives to raise the consciousness of another group of people. They did this in a non-violent manner, but were assisted in their efforts by the Black Power Movement started by such groups as the Black Panthers, and the Civil Rights Movement led by the Southern Christian Leadership Conference, The Student Non-violence Coordinating Committee, The Mississippi Freedom Democratic Party and other organizations.

Beginning with the Niagara and Marcus Garvey Black Nationalist Movements in the 1920s, to the Student Non-Violent Coordination Committee (SNCC), National Association for the Advancement of Colored People (NAACP), Black Panther and Black Muslim political and revolutionary movements in the 50s and 60s, America was about to become a showcase of international attention due to the inherent and pervasive institutional racism and classicism that existed, and still exists in this country.

Men and women of courage, compassion, and vision such as Rosa Parks, Medgar Evers, Malcolm X, A. Phillip Randolph, W.E.B Dubois, Booker T Washington, Paul Robeson, Sojourner Truth, Julian Bond, Mary M. Bethune, Dr. King, Bob Moses, Harriet Tubman, Ben Chavis, Fannie Lou Hamer, Victoria Gray Adams, Annie Devine, Unita Blackwell, the Wilmington 10, Muhammad Ali, Benjamin Banneker, Joe Louis, and <u>many</u> others were willing to sacrifice themselves and their careers to change the moral fabric of this nation. Through the power of their personalities, America was forced to cease practicing the Apartheid-like Jim Crow laws that ruled most regions of this country, and began the journey of learning a new cognition of equality.

Philosophy

There have been so many important Black philosophers that this book will not pretend to discuss, or list all of those people, especially since many of those people also need to be mentioned in the section on literature. Yet, a few people should be discussed here who are considered to be Civil Rights leaders, but are in essence philosophers.

The Reverend Dr. Martin Luther King, Jr. is probably best known as a civil rights leader who believed that peaceful non-violent resistance was the answer to institutional racism and segregation.

Jim Crow Laws led to non-violent protest marches across America to vocalize and draw attention to the unwillingness of minorities and enlightened whites to tolerate the hands of segregation that paralyzed this country.

Yet, King did not begin his career as a civil rights leader. He was a Christian minister with degrees in divinity and philosophy. The civil rights struggle was something he was thrown into, and did not ask for. He happened to have been pastoring a Church as a young Minister in the same city where protests were beginning to occur.

Other Black leaders decided to make him represent the ministers of the city during some of the protests taking place because he was an outsider, not accountable to the white establishment of the city and therefore not subject to the gossip and jealousy of the other ministers.

An indication of King's philosophical skills is evident in his Letter to Birmingham. In it, he cites the Apostle Paul, Hume the philosopher, Yeshua Ha Messiah (Jesus the Christ), and other great philosophers to make a case in point on the spiritual and ethical justification for non-violent protests against segregation, racism, and violation of individual rights.

If the Emancipation Proclamation set Black America free from physical bondage, then King was a modern-day Moses, a spiritual liberator. He, and persons like Sojourner Truth, helped non-Black America and the world achieve a critical consciousness of truth that would enable Americans to examine themselves more closely.

One of King's greatest talents was his ability to articulate and describe the beauty and the spiritual essence philosophy of southern African Americans. This philosophy includes a belief in the strength of the African American people, a pride in our heritage and the future of the Black family, and a particular belief in the beauty, the elegance, and the ambiance of the African American female.

This sophisticated Southern African-American philosophy gave people of color and African descent, as well as sensitive whites, a sense of hope and well-being for many who were cut off from the economic and social mainstream of society.

Paul Robeson was another intellectual who became involved in the civil rights struggle through chance. He was a star athlete, Phi Beta Kappa at Rutgers, and a graduate of Columbia University Law School. He became an opera star, as well as an internationally recognized

Shakespearean actor whose interpretation of Othello on stage became the definitive version to which all others would be compared.

Yet oppression and strife stirred Robeson's soul, and caused him to speak out against the injustices of a supposedly democratic society. Thus, he became involved in The Civil Rights Struggle, and was ultimately black-listed as a communist by the U.S. Government because of remarks he made stating the inability of African Americans to enjoy the privileges of a free society. He, like King, was a talented philosopher/artist who became a civil rights leader more out of necessity than want.

Law

One man who, more than any other, exemplifies the incredible influence that African American lawyers and civil rights activists have had on the legal system and class structure of America is Justice Thurgood Marshall. He was the first, and for many years the only, Black Supreme Court Justice in this nation's history (he announced his retirement in the spring of 1991).

Justice Marshall is one of the great legal scholars of this era, and during his tenure at the Supreme Court, the highest-ranking government official of African American descent. He could have easily concentrated on building a career in law in the Black community, but chose instead to spend much of his adulthood arguing before the Supreme Court several of the most important legal cases in American history.

In the famous case of Brown versus the Board of Education, the Supreme Court handed down a ruling as to the constitutionality of segregation in public schools, especially when those segregated black schools were found to lack the same educational resources as the white schools.

By winning those cases, Marshall and the team of lawyers from the NAACP who worked with him including Harvard Professor Derrick Bell, eventually changed the class structure of this country. Public transportation and public buildings and schools became open to the entire society in the 1960s, and Blacks and other people of color in this country are now able to vote without fear of harassment and discrimination thanks to activists such as those in the Mississippi Democratic Freedom Party who challenged the all-white seating of the Congressional delegation to the Democratic National Convention in 1964. Their efforts received notice from the media and the White House, and were the inspiration that led to the passage of the Voters Rights Act passed by Congress in 1965, which guaranteed the right to vote to persons of all colors and educational and economic backgrounds.

Through the passage of this bill and later amendments to come, a range of opportunities became available not only to blacks, but to women and handicapped individuals as well. America became a changed society.

But as Justice Marshall said in an interview before he died, Blacks are not free yet. We still have a hard struggle ahead before all that was sought is accomplished.

Literature

The list of writers who have influenced American literature is so vast that no attempt could be made to list them all here, or explore each of their contributions.

Modern writers of note

American:

- Phyllis Wheatley was born in Senegal. She became a slave in 1761 and was one of the first African-American poets. She wrote neo-classical poems and published them in 1773 in London.

- Arthur Alfonso Schomburg was a collector of books and artifacts. He was president of the American Negro Academy, and famous Black writers such as W.E.B. Dubois and Alain Locke came to him for help in completing their research projects. Schomburg was a major force in documenting the Black contributions to modern civilization, particularly in renaissance Spain, with his discoveries of paintings by Black artists such as Sebastian Gomez and Juan de Pareja, and his interest in the poetry of Juan Latino.

Therefore, I will list some of the literary giants nationally and internationally acclaimed for their creativity, their literary estheticism, and their contribution to aiding all Americans in comprehending and understanding the historical significance of being an American (and of being an American of African descent):

Gwendolyn Brooks, Poet Laureate of Illinois

- Toni Morrison
- Phyllis Wheatley
- Maya Angelou
- James Baldwin
- Amira Baraka
- Richard Wright
- Alain Locke
- Langston Hughes

- Alex Haley
- Addison Gayle
- William E. Burghardt Dubois
- James Weldon Johnson
- Ralph Ellison

African ethnolinguistic influences in the US

This is an area where subtle but enormous influences have been made on American society in general. Common phrases such as "hey man," "what's up," and "what's happening," which were formerly Afro-American phrases, are now American phrases.

What was once ridiculed for being an inappropriate term such as the Afro-American description of itself as Black, instead of Negro, is now an accepted term to use. As Blacks describe themselves and their world with titles of plays such as "for colored girls who have considered suicide / when the rainbow isn't enuf;" these descriptive and ethereal views have caused whites to take more of an esthetic view of their own everyday world. Consider the play called "A Coupla White Chicks Sitting Around Talking."

To give a more descriptive and scholarly discussion of this subject;

1. Transatlantic Slave Trade: The roots of African ethnolinguistic influences in the United States can be traced back to the transatlantic slave trade, which lasted from the 16th to the 19th centuries. Millions of Africans from various ethnic groups and tribes were forced to come to the Americas, and they brought with them different languages and cultural norms.

2. Creole Languages: During the slave trade, African slaves were forced to communicate with each other and with their European captors, leading to the development of Creole languages. Creoles

are languages that emerge from contact between different linguistic groups and often have simplified grammar and vocabulary. In some regions of the Americas, Creole languages with significant African influences developed, such as Gullah in the southeastern United States. Remnants of the Creole languages can be found throughout the SE areas of the US, particularly in places like New Orleans and Southeastern Louisiana where the slaves had to learn to communicate with the French landowners.

3. African American Vernacular English (AAVE): After the abolition of slavery, African Americans faced segregation and discrimination, which led to the development of distinct speech patterns as a form of identity and resistance. African American Vernacular English (AAVE), commonly known as Ebonics, emerged as a unique linguistic variety with African and other non-standard English influences.

4. Migration and Urbanization: In the 20th century, the Great Migration brought millions of African Americans from the rural South to urban centers in the North and West. This mass migration contributed to the spread and evolution of AAVE across different regions in the United States.

5. Sociolinguistics and Dialectology: Linguists began studying AAVE in the mid-20th century, recognizing it as a distinct and systematic linguistic variety with its own rules and patterns. Sociolinguistic research has since shed light on the cultural, social, and historical factors that have shaped AAVE, and its use in various communities. Because Hip Hop music and Rap music have become so universal, several elements of AAVE have made their way into the vernacular of young white Americans who often imitate in their music, and

social media posts elements of Ebonics that were meant to be used by Black Americans to communicate with each other.

6. Linguistic Diversity and Identity: The African ethnolinguistic influences on the US are just one part of the country's rich linguistic diversity. Many African American communities have retained elements of their African heritage through language, cultural practices, and particularly through music spreading elements of ebonics in stylized spoken word, poetry, and songs contributing to the overall musical and artistic cultural mosaic of the United States.

It is essential to recognize and celebrate the linguistic diversity that exists within the United States, including the influences of African ethnolinguistic heritage, as it reflects the country's historical and cultural evolution.

Sports/Entertainment

From Jesse Owens to Muhammad Ali, and Jackie Robinson to Michael Jordan, Flo Jo and Jackie Kersee Joyner, African Americans have dominated and soared to great heights in the field of sports in the 20th and 21st centuries. In the music industry, a myriad of multi-talented performers and mega stars such as Marvin Gaye, James Brown, Little Richard, Michael Jackson, Stevie Wonder, Lionel Richie, Prince, and more have been able to influence, and in some cases, dominate many parts of the music/entertainment industry. Also, one can not deny an extensive and ongoing influence of the music genre known as Hip Hop and Rap with all their iterations. The year 2023 marks what many Hip Hop artists consider to be, and celebrate, the 50th anniversary of Hip Hop. This music form can be heard from the clubs of Johannesburg South Africa, to restaurants playing this music form in Red Square facing the Capital Building in Moscow. It literally has become the music of the people around the world, and is one of the more imitated and duplicated music forms on the Planet earth.

Long live Black American music, culture, and pride!!!!!

XXVII

Summary

When the reader finishes this book, I hope that the person comes away with this knowledge:

A certain responsibility exists for scholars to recognize that all societies have the right to feel that their culture has, what I call, its own cultural integrity. Each culture has the right to feel that all people who move into a region where the original inhabitants remain are influenced by the aborigines they live with, regardless of whether or not they migrated in as wanderers or as aggressors.

Another purpose of this book is to dispel the fantasy held by white educators and scholars about who is black and who is not.

It was a commonly accepted theory in the 1800s that even some current theorists believe, that (rather than recognizing the hundreds of cultural groups that exist), there are three races; the Negroid, the Caucasoid, and the Asian races.

With the world so neatly divided between those three groups, they (white scholars) began to categorize the contributions of humanity based on examining which racial groups did what.

Between 1800 and 1900, according to historian and scholar Martin Bernal, an Aryan model of history was created. This model discarded the Greek view of their own past which acknowledges that African Egyptians introduced civilization to Greece. This view was replaced by an Aryan model which states that: Greece became civilized after being conquered by European whites from the north. This model also states that the Egyptians were a non-African people, and later that Ethiopians were a mixed group who could not be seen as connected to tribes who originated in equatorial Africa.

Ethiopians categorized as Negroid were found later by white historians to be responsible for some of the earliest achievements of humanity, and the ancient Egyptians, one of the most famous and creative of tribes, trace their lineage to Sub-Saharan Africa. So what's a scientist to do?

In looking at why each country was picked in the list of countries section, many countries that have a strong African influence were left out. That is not to say that countries in the Caribbean such as the British Virgin Isles, Curacao and Guyana, Venezuela, Saudi Arabia, India, France, Honduras, and many more areas of the world do not have a strong African influence.

The countries that I chose to discuss in this book had an influence that is undeniable, and so significant, that if you took away the African presence in that country, either by taking away the impact Africa had on their history, or the current impact on the culture, it would, in its current form, cease to exist.

Now I would like to briefly discuss this book in terms of its connection to multicultural education.

I hope this book will become a part of multicultural education, and a necessary tool for educators and political activists who believe that there is a critical need to increase self-esteem for children of color. Hopefully, this book will help reduce the crippling effects, that the curriculums currently being used in the public and private schools, are having on the minds of young children of color in this country.

Multicultural education is necessary to assist students in being able to critically reflect on issues of social justice and classism in America.

By redefining their history, and designing new educational institutions that teach such philosophies, these newly empowered students will be able to develop strong academic skills. These students can make a greater contribution to their own communities, as well as compete more effectively in the business and academic world of an America that views people of color as members of oppressed communities.

Another reason why multicultural education is needed is because students empowered with this philosophical approach can make a contribution to the future curriculums used in the next century. When students are trained in this multicultural academic tradition of excellence that I envision, they will become Neo-African American Griots who will rewrite and redefine current Eurocentric histories currently taught in public and private schools. This will assist African American, Native American, and Native Central and South American students in being able to promote and bequeath to future generations knowledge of their historical, oral, and written traditions of excellence.

Those great academic traditions of Africa have produced historical legacies of great civilizations that have existed for thousands of years before Western civilizations began. They have been diminished and discarded as colonialization, and later assimilation, by people of color has taken place in Western societies.

Another important goal of multicultural education is to prepare students to begin evaluating the important events of the 20th century from an Afrocentric/Native American perspective, so as to assist the students in identifying the critical issues of this century, and examine what conclusions could be drawn from analyzing important events from a non-western, non-Eurocentric perspective.

By doing this historical evaluation, students can then prepare new bodies of literature on the successes and failures of the human species in this era. This information can be used to help future educators assess and learn from the mistakes of the past.

The goals of the section on African art are to assist students in increasing their math skills, and visual spatial relationship skills, and develop a knowledge and comprehension of geometric and concentric design and African art as it relates to the academic discipline of philosophy.

This will assist the student in having an increased awareness and respect for his or her culture, and increase his or her analytical and literacy skills.

XXVIII

African Art Essay

The discussion on African art is important to me. I feel that not nearly enough critical analysis has been done in the area of comparative studies on African art, and African art in the Diaspora.

Hopefully, this book will inspire the general public information to investigate the profound influence African art has had on some of Europe's finest artists, and also show in an easy-to-read fashion, the incredible complexity and highly sophisticated manner in which African artists express complex philosophical concepts.

In conclusion, I hope that by mentioning the beauty and sophistication of that art form, students can examine African art, and this discussion of African art will hopefully assist students in becoming more empowered. That can happen if students learn the role and complexity of art forms from other parts of the world, and Africa in particular, and will gain knowledge, strength, and spiritual power from their studies. This analysis of African art will help the student understand the connection between art and philosophy, and how other non-western societies express their world views. By studying this information, the student will gain a new conception of philosophy, and can then begin a didactic epistemological journey.

By explaining the influence of West and Central African art on the geometric continuity of Afro-American, Afro-Brazilian, Afro-Caribbean, and European art, the students can increase their respect for the intricate manner in which other cultures create art, and hone their skills as young African art-driven philosophers. This has powerful implications for multicultural education.

Another point to be made about the last section of the book is that I do not spend a great deal of time documenting or listing supportive evidence for historical facts that are commonly accepted as being true. For example, it is commonly accepted that Timbuctu is in Africa, the Moors built the Alhambra Palace and traveled as far north as the British Isles.

What is hotly contested heavily by European, African American Afrocentric scholars, and some lay people, is the ethnic origin of those groups. That is why I spend a considerable amount of time at the beginning of the book discussing this topic, and reiterating over and over again - the people discussed in the book are direct descendants of tribes from equatorial Africa (below the Sahara desert, toward the equator), where people have dark complexions and West and East African facial features and characteristics. It is true in the case of the Moors that lighter-skinned Arabs also came up to Europe. But this does not negate the irrefutable evidence that darker Africans who are originally from the motherland also came to Spain and Southern Europe since they left sculptured figures of their representations, which in some cases show individuals with pigmy-like features.

As time goes on, the voices of the next generation of writers are now being heard. Those voices of empowerment include Africologists/Afrocentric scholars such as Dr. Cecil Gray, Dr. Charles Finch (already an accomplished author), Dr. Kamau Johnson, Charlin Diver, a Native American educator from the Minnesota Chippewa Tribe who was on the faculty at Fond du Lac Community College Center, and Tamara Johnson and other scholars trained at the University of Virginia, Rutgers, Virginia Commonwealth University, Yale, Hampton University, Stanford, Temple University, Spellman, Howard, Morehouse, and many other schools.

Those neo-African and Native American Griots articulate and describe their heritage. They give credence to the strength of early African civilizations, and discuss the ancient and sophisticated nature of early Native North and Central American civilizations such as the Aztec and the Mayan empires.

Boston historians such as Donna La Rue have begun taking notice of, and making available to the public, research that acknowledges the genealogy of Black slaves in Boston during the Revolutionary War. Ms. La Rue seeks to preserve and document historical information as to where slaves during that time in history were buried.

Another important aim of this kind of book is to inspire and challenge the reader to see the need for more books written that include many perspectives from people of various ethnic religious and cultural backgrounds.

Hopefully, this book will present a perspective that stresses the need for cultural revisionists who will redefine and publish information that has a Neo-African American/Native American perspective on each culture's contribution to herstory/ourstory.

In essence, I hope to share my beliefs through this book.

XXIX

My core beliefs

I believe in the feminine power of the Creator of all things (blessed is She), the unity of the Spirit of Ma'at; I believe in The Mother, the Son (Yeshua Ha Mesiah, the Afro Asiatic one) and the Holy Ghost.

Amon, Blessed be the name of the Creator Amun; Blessed be the name Amen; Blessed is She.

My sheroes of the past and the present - Persons of vision and hope who are an inspiration to me, and should be an inspiration to us all:

Katherine Johnson

Henrietta Lacks

Harriet Tubman

Sojourner Truth

Unita Blackwell

Victoria Gray Adams

Dr. Frances Cress Wesling

Fannie Lou Hamer

Annie Divine

Dr. Marian Wright Edelman

Audrey Anne Robinson (rest in Power), my mother and personal sheroe.

I want to give a shout out to my God Daughters Shinay, Shawna and Shella.

I also want to give a shout out to Nettsaanett Hunt Adams. Keep moving upward and onward.

Thanks to Nehemiah for all your support over the years; my cousins Janice and Regina, love you both dearly.

Also, many props and thanks to Matthew, for making my 35-year vision become a reality.

XXX

ISAIAH 19:19-21

In that day shall there be an altar to the Lord in the midst of the Land of Egypt, and a pillar at the border thereof to the Lord.

And it shall be for a sign and for a witness unto the Lord of Hosts in the Land of Egypt: for they shall cry unto the Lord because of the oppressors, and he shall send them a savior, and a great one, and he shall deliver them.

And the Lord shall be known to Egypt, and the Egyptians shall know the Lord in that day, ... 19:24-25.

In that day shall Israel be the third with Egypt and with Assyria, even a blessing in the midst of the Land: Whom the Lord of hosts shall bless, saying Blessed be Egypt my people, and Assyria the work of my hands, and Israel mine inheritance.

To the reader, a blessing:

THE LOVE THAT COMES FROM WITHIN ME, THAT COMES FROM MY HEART AND SOUL:

I GIVE TO YOU.

End of book.

XXXI

About the Author

Geronimo Robinson is a Harvard and University of Virginia trained-educator who is currently a Guest lecturer with the University of Cyprus Department of Inclusive Education. His lectures at UCY are on the "intersectionality of the civil rights movement, and the fight for independence and self-determination for persons with Mental Health Issues. He has published several articles in the disabilities field including an article entitled: The Impact of Race, Poverty, and Ethnicity on Services for Persons With Mental Disabilities: A Call for Cultural Competence, and another article named: Quilomboos, Black Nationalism, and Self-Determination for Persons with Intellectual Disabilities: A Psychohistorical Perspective.

Mr. Robinson is the former president of the Municipal Opera Company of Baltimore, one of a handful of American Opera companies and major American cultural institutions founded by Black Americans.

Mr. Robinson chaired the Multicultural Special Interest Group in the late 90s and early 2000s in the American Association on Intellectual & Developmental Disabilities (AAIDD). This committee was responsible for designing and advocating for changes in how individuals with disabilities are assessed clinically so that minority groups, and particularly Black American male children, would not disproportionately be given a label of mild intellectual disability.

Mr. Robinson is the former Chair of the Diversity Committee, for the City of Alexandria Community Services Board.

Mr. Robinson is the former President of the Black Student Union at the Harvard University Graduate School of Education. While in that position in 1992, Mr. Robinson co-founded the Coalition, an umbrella organization consisting of leaders of all black organizations at Harvard University working together to collectively call for change in the treatment of women of color faculty at Harvard. The goal of the Coalition was to stop discrimination against African American female faculty at the Harvard School of Law, who at that time in 1992, were unable to become tenured professors. Due to the efforts of the Coalition and organizations around the world, Harvard University did finally change its policy, and hired more female and women of color, in particular as professors, at various schools within the University, and allowed Black women to become tenured professors at the Law school by the end of the decade.

Mr. Robinson also received a master's degree from the University of Virginia where he studied the aesthetics of African art, with an emphasis on the sculpted figures of the Luba and Kuba tribes of the Republic of the Congo.

Mr. Robinson was invited to speak at the Mary McLeod Bethune House in Washington DC on Civil Rights Icon Victoria Grey Adams, co-founder of the Mississippi Freedom Democratic Party, and showed excerpts of her interview in the PBS video, "Standing on my Sisters Shoulders," February 2007.

Mr. Robinson was also invited to join the late legendary Civil Rights leader Dr. Dorothy Height, for High Tea as she reflected on the role of women, and the National Council of Negro Women in the March on Washington in 1963. This event took place on Saturday, August 23, 2008, and was hosted at the National Council on Negro Women (NCNW) Headquarters, 633 Pennsylvania Avenue, NW Washington, DC.

In 2012, at a ceremony in Charlotte NC, Mr. Robinson was awarded the title of Fellow with the American Association on Intellectual and Developmental Disabilities (AAIDD) to honor Mr. Robinson for his work in the Republic of Botswana. Mr. Robinson developed a nationwide program where his non-profit, For Those In Need, Inc., collaborated with the Department of Social Services for the Republic of Botswana, to train Case Management and Social Service staff on how to develop clinical protocols to deliver a sequence of five separate, but overlapping, phases of activity including: assessment and screening for orphans and vulnerable children OVC. The goal was to develop and implement services, and to develop and monitor a program evaluation process. The project was able to provide support for more than 20,000 children in Botswana during a five year period.

Mr. Robinson was invited to a reception at Cypriot Embassy in February 2016 by His Excellency, Ambassador Chacalli, Cyprus Ambassador to the US. The purpose of the reception was to thank myself, and the Delegation I led in 2000, for conducting workshops in April, 2000 at the University of Cyprus onsite, as well as conducting a teleconference at the University of Cyprus in April 2015.

Aa a member of the Fairfax County Diversity, Equity and inclusion Committee, Mr. Robinson recorded a video that is posted on the

Fairfax County YouTube Channel on Black Men's Health, sponsored by the Fairfax County Department of Public Health Be Well Program.

Mr. Robinson was invited to a reception at the home of the Botswana Ambassador to the US in Potomac, MD in June 2011, celebrating a concert held by The United Congregational Church of Southern Africa Broadhurst choir at Howard University.

Mr. Robinson was an invited guest at the Madagascar Embassy, occurring in June of 1999, for a meeting with the President of the Virginia Chapter of the National Alliance on Mental Illness, and the Madagascar Ambassador to the US, located on Embassy Row in Northwest Washington, DC.

Mr. Robinson conducted two lectures at the Corcoran Museum in downtown Washington, DC on November 18, 2008, on the complex and intricate expression of spiritual, matriarchal and legal concepts found in the Luba and Dogon sculpted figures and mask in Central Africa.

Mr. Robinson has spent most of his adult life traveling to countries in Southern Europe, Northern Africa, the Caribbean, and South America observing the influence of the African Diaspora on the development of early human civilizations and cultures. A highlight for Mr. Robinson was being named a recipient of the Smithsonian's list of bibliographies and journal articles on all things African. It was a compilation/list of any and all books or articles written about topics related to African history and culture generated by authors from all continents, and distributed to only 200 scholars around the world.

www.ingramcontent.com/pod-product-compliance
Lightning Source LLC
Chambersburg PA
CBHW060104170726
48004CB00013B/378